We Wish you
a Happy Birthday.
We wish you to
become no 1. in
Tennis.
        Love
    Fran
Aunty Chris, Uncle
        Tom
Christopher +
Trevor.

5/21/88

DESIGN B

DESIGN B

How to Play Tennis in the Zone

Scott Ford

ICARUS PRESS
South Bend, Indiana
1984

DESIGN B
Copyright © 1984 by Scott Ford

1   2   3   4   5   6   87   86   85   84

Icarus Press, Inc.
P.O. Box 1225
South Bend, Indiana 46624

Library of Congress Cataloging in Publication Data

Ford, Scott, 1948–
  Design B: how to play tennis in the zone.

  Includes index.
  1. Tennis. I. Title.
GV995.F638   1984   796.342'2   84–4677
ISBN 0–89651–153–7

To DJ and Barb

CONTENTS

1

The Shield

I AM A TENNIS PRO. I TEACH PEOPLE HOW TO PLAY TENNIS. It's a crazy job, really. You see all kinds on the tennis court; every shape, every size, every color. All of them running around out there trying to knock a little yellow ball back and forth across the net. Some of them do it with flair, some with unorthodox efficiency, some of them even do it with their eyes closed.

For a long time I taught people how to play tennis in the traditional manner. I showed them how to take their backswing just so, how to move their feet, how to swing their racket this way to produce one effect, that way to produce another. Sound fundamentals, the basic turn-step-swing approach to playing the game.

After awhile this got boring. Turn-step-swing, turn-step-swing, day-in, day-out, after eighteen years the traditional approach to teaching tennis was driving me crazy. And then one day, quite by accident, I chanced onto something special, something extraordinary.

It happened while I was watching several of my students playing in a club mixed doubles tournament. As I watched I observed something similar in each of their games. It had nothing to do with technique; in fact, each player was progressing normally in their technical skills. Instead, what I observed dealt with the area of space we tennis pros call the "Hitting Zone" or, more exactly, the "Contact Zone."

It was a simple observation: When contact occurred *inside* the imaginary boundaries of the contact zone, the results were usually good. When contact occurred *outside* the boundaries of the contact zone, the results were usually bad.

That's it. That was my observation. Contact inside the contact zone — Positive. Contact outside the contact zone — Negative. Not exactly a profound observation, but it did start me wondering about the relationship of the contact zone to the entire stroke.

As a teaching pro I had always mentioned the contact zone in my lessons, defining it as the general area in which the racket should contact the ball. But as I watched my students play, I was surprised to see how irregularly they were actually contacting the ball within the contact zone. More surprising was the consistency of negative contact once the ball got past this imaginary zone. Even the best technical player on the court had little success once the ball got past his contact zone.

Conversely, whenever the ball was struck within the imaginary boundaries of the player's contact zone, regardless of the technique employed, the results were markedly improved. More often than not, the ball was contacted solidly and the placement was accurate.

So why weren't my students contacting every ball within the imaginary boundaries of their contact zones? It was a question that perplexed me; so the next day when I went to the courts with a friend, I was determined to look for a different way of defining this imaginary contact zone.

I had been having problems with my own game, in particular, my mid-court volley, and I wondered if this contact zone error might be the cause of my problem.

As my friend and I started volleying back and forth from mid-court, I immediately noticed several balls zipping past my contact zone. This bothered me. Here I was, the big tennis pro. I wasn't supposed to make such an obvious error. But I was, and although many of my shots went back, I felt cramped, late, and, in general, very ineffective.

But knowing the cause did not solve my problem, mostly because this contact zone was nothing more than an imaginary field located somewhere out there in front of me. There was nothing substantial, no visible object to mark its location at all times.

So I did something simple. I pretended I had an "Invisible Shield," like a large pane of Plexiglas, stretched across the court in front of me, right where my contact zone should be.

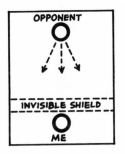

As silly as this seemed at first, it also made pretty good sense. Any ball hit in my direction would eventually touch a point somewhere along this imaginary shield, and if my racket arrived at the "Touchpoint" simultaneously with the ball, then, logically, I would be contacting the ball in my contact zone.

I had no idea what would happen, but I wanted to observe what it felt like to let nothing get past my Invisible Shield. That way, I knew I would be contacting the ball in the contact zone, and, I hoped, my mid-court game would improve.

We began again, and I noticed that I saw the ball clearly when my friend hit it, but it was a blur when it got to my Invisible Shield. I could not refocus my eyes fast enough to see the ball clearly in both places.

This struck me as backwards. If I were going to see the ball at all, the most logical place for me to see it clearly should be at *my* point of contact, not my opponent's. So I decided to try something different. Knowing the shield represented my contact zone, it seemed reasonable that the Touchpoint on my Shield would represent my point of contact, and *that* was the place I wanted to see the ball clearly; the Touchpoint on my Invisible Shield. If I could see it there, then I was seeing it where it counted the most —at *my* point of contact.

So as we started again, I began "looking for the Touchpoint" on my Invisible Shield rather than "watching the ball" along its flight line. This went completely against the traditional way I had learned to "watch the ball," but I was determined to give it a try.

It took a few volleys to acquaint my eyes with the difference in visual focus, then, almost suddenly, it started to work. I couldn't believe it! Instead of the ball starting out clearly, then blurring as it got to my Shield, it was starting out as a peripheral blur, then gathering in clarity as it got closer to my Shield. The feeling was very different; everything was reversed. But I was seeing the ball clearly at *my* point of contact. As a result, my volley took a dramatic leap in efficiency.

More amazing than the improvement in my volley was

what happened when the exchange ended. You see, when we finally stopped, I had to shake myself out of the daze I was in. Whatever I had been doing on the court had put me into a trance. It was a strange sensation, but it was a sensation I had felt before, on those rare occasions when, for some inexplicable reason, everything seemed to come together on the court. When I was playing in the juniors we had a name for this trance-like sensation, and although it was none-too scientific, it still seemed to convey the feeling. We called it "Zoning," and while we all knew it had something to do with concentration, we weren't exactly sure what it was, nor did we care. It worked, and that was good enough for us. Whatever we were doing when we were "in the zone," however strange the sensation, we went with it. As a result, we usually amazed ourselves, not to mention the effect it had on our opponents!

I tried this Invisible Shield idea again and again. Every time the same thing happened — I zoned! And all I was doing was making sure nothing got past my Invisible Shield.

Needless to say, I was excited! "What's going on?" I asked myself. Was this a fluke, or had I actually chanced onto something important? What was it about a silly Invisible Shield that brought on this strange sensation? Questions started flying through my mind. The most obvious being: Will it work for anyone else? There was always the possibility that I was just having one of those days. But deep inside I knew this was different. I could actually switch back and forth from the normal way I felt to this strange, trance-like state. All I had to do was stop "watching the ball," and start "looking for the Touchpoint on my Invisible Shield." Best of all, it was working!

Even my friend noticed the difference. "What's with you?" he asked. So I showed him the Invisible Shield.

His initial reaction — hesitancy. But after a few remarks about my mental health, he gave it a try.

Like me, it took him a few minutes to get used to the

change in visual focus. Then, almost suddenly, the same transformation took place. My friend was "in the zone"!

"Wow!" he said when the exchange ended. "That was weird!"

"Wow!" and "Weird!," these two exclamations define the basic paradox I was facing with the Shield. It worked, and worked very well, but there was still that strange sensation. Some people said, "Wow!" and liked it. Others said, "Wow!" and didn't. The important thing to me was that they all said, "Wow!," whether or not they liked the strange sensation was a matter of personal choice. The fact remained that whenever someone tried the Shield, the transformation in their game was immediate and dramatic. Some people, however, did not want to change the way they normally felt on the court, even if it meant improving their play.

This was confusing to me. Personally I felt very comfortable with this sensation, but I had no explanation for what it was or why it worked, which posed a problem. Imagine telling a 40-year-old housewife to pretend she has an Invisible Shield in front of her, and when she asks why, coming up with a highly definitive explanation: "Because it makes you zone."

I found out rapidly that today's tennis player wants something a little more conclusive than "It makes you zone."

So I sat down to figure out this Shield idea. What was this strange, almost hypnotic sensation, and why did it help me play so much better?

Finding the answers was like unraveling a mystery.

2

The Visual Pattern

THE FOUNDATION OF DESIGN B IS A VISUAL TRACKING PAT-
tern, but a tracking pattern of unusual nature in that it
does not involve "watching the ball" in the traditional sense.
Instead, Design B uses a completely different visual tracking pattern designed to perform one task — to track down
the most important visual event that occurs on the court.
The event of the ball and your racket coming together at a
common point in space and time — Whacko! The Contact
Event.

The Contact Event

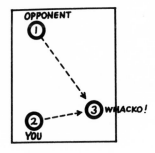

Design B uses a slightly altered approach to tracking down the Contact Event. You see, as far as your eyes are concerned, "watching the ball" is only one approach to tracking down contact. It is the traditional approach. The approach dictated by logic.

Logically, by tracking the ball along its flightline your eyes will eventually reach Point 3—the Contact Point. Whacko!

There is, however, an alternate approach to tracking down the Contact Event. An approach also dictated by logic, although, at first, this alternate approach seems totally illogical. And for good reason—the first step in the visual pattern of Design B: *Don't*, I repeat, *don't* watch the ball!

An Imaginary Visual Situation

Perhaps the easiest way to understand the visual pattern of Design B is through an imaginary visual situation.

Imagine this: You are standing in a large living room, looking through a large picture window located approximately arm's length in front of you. Outside, a young boy throws a snowball at your picture window.

Here's how it looks in diagram form:

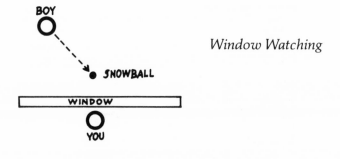

Window Watching

This visual situation is similar to the one you face on a tennis court.

Diagram A   *Diagram B*

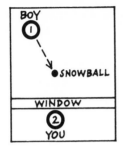   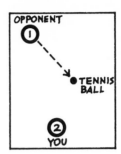

When seen side-by-side, the similarities between Diagram A and Diagram B are self-evident. The only thing missing in Diagram B is a picture window. Everything else is essentially the same — objects of similar size, traveling similar flight lines, at similar speeds. Both objects destined for contact.

If you use your imagination, not only can you supply the motion to these motionless pictures, you can also imagine a third diagram. The one you get when you superimpose Diagram A atop Diagram B. The one you get when you imagine an Invisible Shield spanning the court in front of you at the depth of your contact zone.

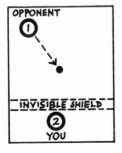

Diagram C

The trick to understanding Diagram C is simple. On a tennis court the Invisible Shield isn't really there, but the contact zone is. And that's what the visual pattern of Design B is all about: watching the contact zone instead of watching the ball.

Sounds illogical, doesn't it? Who in his right mind would consciously choose to watch an area of open space as the ball comes toward it? After all, that's what you are doing when you visualize an imaginary Shield across your contact zone. You are literally fixing the focus of your eyes on nothing!

You might say, it's like watching a window. But in this visual situation there is a lot more to window watching than first meets the eye.

Window Watching

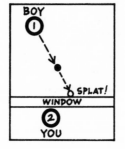

Diagram A

Consider this: In Diagram A you are involved in a visual contest. A contest between a moving object and your eyes. Physical movement versus visual countermovement.

The object of this contest is simple: There will be a Contact Event in this visual situation, an event in which the snowball and the window come together at a contact point. SPLAT! The Contact Event.

The object of this game is to see the Contact Event as clearly as possible, to track down the Contact Event with your eyes. In this game, you win when you "see the splat."

Rules of play?

None. You can look for contact any way you want.

Sounds like an easy game, doesn't it? All you do is stand behind your window and watch as the boy picks up a handful of snow, mashes it into a perfectly round object, glances disdainfully in your direction, and whips you an air-mail delivery. Your objective: to see the splat clearly.

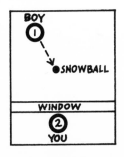

So far, in this visual situation, nothing resembling a splat has taken place. The Contact Event has yet to occur. However, the two objects destined for contact are clearly visible in this diagram. The snowball and the window. Both objects play an important role in the Contact Event, but the Contact Event itself, the SPLAT, will not be visible until these two objects come together at a Contact Point. A Contact Point that will be located somewhere along the surface of the window. In fact, no matter how many snowballs the boy throws at your window, it is safe to assume that the Contact Event will *always* take place along the surface of your window. Unless the kid is a rubber arm.

Question: If the most important event in this visual contest, the Contact Event, *always* takes place along the surface of the window, then why not watch the surface of the
window for contact?

After all, the window is stationary, which means the
depth of contact is always the same; a visual constant.
Everything else is moving; visual variables.

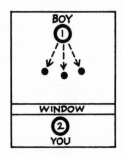

The boy is in motion—a minor variable.

The snowball is in motion—a major variable.

Your eyes are in motion—a biggy.

The window is stationary—a constant. A visual constant among all those variables. So why not focus on the
constant instead of the variable? Why not focus on the
window instead of the snowball? It's a lot easier to keep a
stationary object in focus than it is to keep a moving object
in focus. Particularly an object moving as fast as a
snowball, or a tennis ball.

Besides, by fixing the focus of your eyes on the window,
you are effectively "pre-focusing" on the depth of contact,
and, logically, if your eyes are focused on the window,
then any object coming *toward* the window will also be
coming *into* focus.

Which is exactly what happens! With your eyes focused
on the window, the snowball *begins* its flight line as a

visual blur, a moving object that is out of focus. But as it nears the *end* of its flight line, the snowball comes *into* your field of focus, and the closer it gets to the window, the more it gathers in focal clarity. So instead of seeing the snowball clearly at the *beginning* of its flight line, you simply fix your focus on the window and track down the *end* of its flight line.

Guess what you see there? SPLAT! The Contact Event. And you see it very clearly.

What does this prove? Only that there is more than one way to track down the Contact Event in this visual situation. You can focus on the snowball as it comes toward your window, or you can focus on your window as the snowball comes toward it.

There's a big difference there. Two completely different visual tracking patterns, both are designed to track down the most important event in the contest—the Contact Event. The question is, which way do you see the SPLAT more clearly? By watching the snowball, or by watching the window?

Prefocus Versus Refocus

With the window located approximately arm's-length in front of you, it is safe to assume that the Contact Event

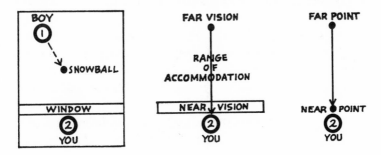

will always occur in your *near* field of vision. In other words, to see the SPLAT clearly your eyes must eventually be focused for near vision.

Watching the snowball along its flight line from far point to near point is actually a combination of two eye movements working together simultaneously. These eye movements are called "convergence" and "accommodation." Convergence deals with the rotational movements of the eye as you track the snowball along its flight line, while accommodation deals with the lens of the eye refocusing from far vision to near vision to accommodate for the changing focal depth of the snowball's flight line.

When you "prefocus" on the window, however, this accommodation process is completed *before* the snowball is thrown. In other words, by fixing the focus of your eyes on the window, no refocusing from far vision to near vision is necessary. Your eyes are already focused for near vision. You might say: "Prefocusing eliminates refocusing." And when you eliminate the accommodation movement, you are eliminating a major visual variable in this situation.

Think of it this way: When you "watch the ball," or in this case, when you "watch the snowball," your focus is in a state of flux, constantly changing, refocusing, a visual variable.

But when you "watch the window" your focus is stationary, fixed, a visual constant defined by a simple equation:

Depth of Focus =
Depth of Contact

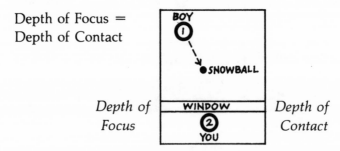

Depth of Focus   *Depth of Contact*

The visual tracking pattern of Design B simulates this' visual equation. By visualizing a Shield across your contact zone, you are effectively creating a visual constant, a fixed focus. Your very own window on the tennis court.

Visual Mimicry

The visual tracking pattern of Design B is one of visual mimicry. Mimicry in that visualizing an imaginary Shield across your contact zone simulates the focusing pattern created when you fix the focus of your eyes on a window.

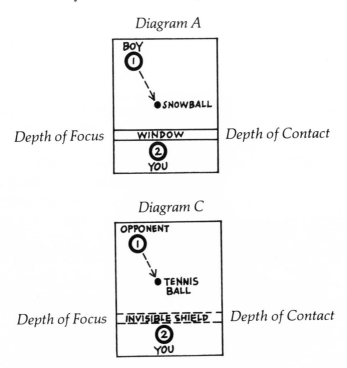

Diagram A

Diagram C

Both focusing patterns complete the visual equation: "Depth of focus equals depth of contact." Both focusing

patterns create a visual constant, a fixed depth of focus. And just as fixing your focus on the "window" alters your visual awareness of the snowball, so, too, fixing your focus on the contact zone alters your visual awareness of the tennis ball. In fact, you get the same visual reversal; the tennis ball *begins* its flight line as a visual blur, a moving object that is out of focus. But as it nears the *end* of its flight line, the contact zone, it begins to increase in clarity. Which is very nice, since the contact zone is where you would like to see the ball the best.

Two Tracking Patterns

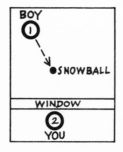

V-Trak

The traditional pattern of tracking down the Contact Event in this visual situation is to watch the snowball along its flight line until it gets to the window — SPLAT!

This "tracking pattern" of watching the snowball from far point to near point is a "Variable Focus Tracking Pattern." In other words, when you watch the snowball along its flight line from far point to near point, not only must you "track" the ball with the rotational movements of your eyes (convergence), you must also "refocus" your eyes from far vision to near vision (accommodation); the lens of

the eye is in a variable state, constantly refocusing to accommodate for the changing focal depth of the snowball's
flight line. Thus, watching the snowball is a variable focus
tracking pattern — V-Trak.

F-Trak

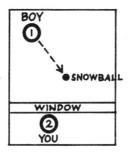

Design B uses an altered tracking pattern with the same
visual objective — to track down the Contact Event with
your eyes. But instead of tracking down the Contact Event
by watching the snowball as it moves toward the window
(V-Trak), the visual pattern in Design B is to watch the
window as the snowball moves toward it. This is a "Fixed
Focus Tracking Pattern" (F-Trak).

This fixed focus tracking pattern suggests that you can
use your eyes differently on a tennis court. You do not, in
fact, have to "watch the ball" to track down the Contact
Event. You can also visualize a Shield across your contact
zone, and "look for the touchpoint." This is a fixed focus
tracking pattern. The lens of the eye prefocused on the
contact zone. Accommodation complete. Prefocusing
eliminates refocusing

The Touchpoint in Diagram A is Point 3. The point
where the snowball comes together with the window —
SPLAT!

The Contact Event is located at the Touchpoint.

In Diagram C, Point 3 is also the Touchpoint. The point

where the tennis ball comes together with your Invisible Shield. Or, more exactly, the point where the tennis ball first enters your contact zone.

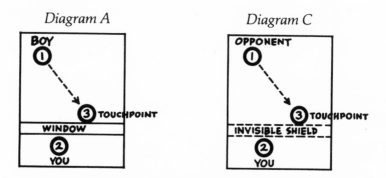

Diagram A   Diagram C

The visual tracking pattern of Design B is meant to track down this Touchpoint as efficiently as possible, and to track it down for one very specific reason: so you can hit it with your racket.

Which, in a nutshell, defines the physical pattern of Design B. A physical pattern to co-host in the logic of Design B. You see, where the visual tracking pattern of Design B says: *Don't* watch the ball. The physical pattern says: Don't hit it either. Hit something else.

Hit the Touchpoint!

3
The Physical Pattern

THE GAME OF TENNIS IS TRADITIONALLY VIEWED AS A CONTEST between the ball, a moving object, and you, another moving object; only on a tennis court, your movements are called countermovements. And they are part of the fundamental confrontation in the game. The movement of the ball versus your countermovements to intercept the ball. Movement versus countermovement; competition in base form. The object of this competition: contact.

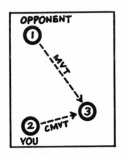

This is a diagram of the fundamental competitive sequence in tennis: the Contact Sequence. As you can see this contact sequence begins with the movement of the ball along its flight line, followed by your countermovements along the line of interception, ending with contact, the event of the ball and your racket coming together at a common point in space and time.

Movement → Countermovement → Contact; the Contact Sequence.

If you take a closer look at this contact sequence you can see that *you* play the role of countermovement, and your objective as countermovement is not simply contact, but Positive Contact. Contacting a tennis ball with a racket is easy. The big question is whether that Contact Event is Positive or Negative. Contact (+) or Contact (−).

Negative Contact, as you know, is a drag. It causes a variety of negative responses, racket throttling, cursing, self-abuse. The list goes on.

Positive Contact, on the other hand, gets a positive response: "Yippee!," and Positive Contact is what the physical pattern of Design B is all about. Let's fact it. If you make Positive Contact one more time than your opponent, then you take home the trophy. So the big question becomes how do you make Positive Contact?

The Positive Contact Zone

If you have ever hit tennis balls against a wall, or a backboard, or a garage door (where I learned to play), then you know what it is like to meet your match. The wall always wins.

In all my years of tennis I have never beaten the wall. Nor have I ever let it bother me. The way I figure it, Big

Bill Tilden never beat the wall. Don Budge never beat the wall. Laver, Ashe, Goolagong, Billie Jean — all great players, competitors of the highest calliber. Yet every time they play against the wall, guess who always wins?

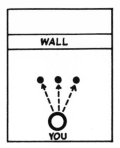

The point is, if you are looking for some solid competition, you don't have to go on the international circuit to find it. Just find the nearest wall and you are looking at the best competition in the world. And you don't need an invitation to play. The wall is always ready for a game.

In this diagram you get to pick your opponent. You can see your opponent as the wall, or, if you use your imagination, you can see your opponent as an imaginary character standing just *behind* the wall. You can't really see this mystery opponent, but you know one thing — he certainly is effective! It's uncanny! The ball always comes back. You might say your mystery opponent always makes Positive Contact. It makes you wonder what he is doing that you are not. Of course, it's easy enough to find out. After all, it's your imagination, and to see what your mystery opponent is doing behind the wall, you need simply make the wall transparent; something akin to Plexiglas.

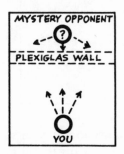

There! That's better. Now you've got something going for you, because behind your transparent wall stands the player who always makes Positive Contact. In fact, your mystery opponent plays his entire game behind a "see-through" Positive Contact Zone. And what you can learn from this imaginary player can help you understand the physical pattern of Design B, a physical pattern *not* based on the ball, but based on the location of your Positive Contact Zone.

In this diagram your part is easy. All you do is initiate the movement of the ball toward the wall—Whacko! End of role. Your part is over. All you do now is relax and use your imagination. The rest of the contact sequence is between the ball and your mystery opponent. Movement versus countermovement: fundamental competition.

As usual, the character of movement is being played by the tennis ball. The character of countermovement, however, is being played by your imaginary opponent, an opponent with a definite gift for Positive Contact. Every time the ball gets to his Positive Contact Zone—Whacko! Positive Contact. The ball keeps coming back.

Give him your best serve—Whacko! The ball comes back.

Slice one down his alley—Whacko! The ball comes back.

Topspin, cross court—Whacko! The ball comes back.

Whew! This guy is really good! No wonder he always wins. He never misses. Which makes your mystery opponent pretty tough to beat. But don't feel bad. Nobody beats the wall, or the imaginary player behind the wall. Besides, the idea is not to beat this player, but to see how he plays. Remember, the wall is transparent—Plexiglas. You can actually see this player demonstrating what he does best, and what he does best is get the ball back. You might say he completes every contact sequence with Positive Contact.

Movement → Countermovement → Contact (+).

Now ask yourself this: Do you complete every contact sequence with Positive Contact? Or do you sometimes get this:

Movement → Countermovement → Contact (−).

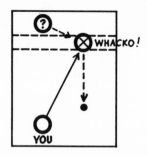

Here's another imaginary situation, only this situation is about what happens when a dirty tennis ball comes together with a clean Plexiglas wall.

For one thing, the ball bounces back: Contact (+).

For another, it leaves a smudge on the Plexiglas. "X" marks the spot of the smudge, and your imaginary opponent hates smudges. He likes to keep his Plexiglas wall as clean as possible. So what does he do? He takes his trusty, graphite smudge-swatter, stands about arm's-lenth behind his Plexiglas wall, and proceeds to swat smudges, that's what!

And he's very good at it! Those smudges don't have a chance against this mystery opponent. Right when they get to his Positive Contact Zone—Whacko! He swats 'em.

The crazy thing is, every time he swats a smudge on his Plexiglas wall, his smudge-swatter also contacts the tennis ball in his Positive Contact Zone.

Result: Whacko! Contact (+). The ball comes back. Now it's your problem.

What makes things interesting is that this imaginary player isn't trying to contact the ball! He's only interested in contacting smudges, and he doesn't care how he does it! As long as the flat side of his smudge-swatter arrives at Point X simultaneously with the ball, he's happy!

Whacko! One smudge bites the dust.

And if you can see this imaginary player in your mind's eye, moving around behind his Plexiglas wall, swatting smudges, you begin to realize that although you are watching an imaginary character, making imaginary countermovements, those countermovements look suprisingly similar to the ones you see on a tennis court.

Question: If you took away this player's Plexiglas wall and made him play *real* tennis on a *real* tennis court, do you think he would change his style of play?

I don't. Not unless he's a dummy. Why change his style of play when he has never lost a match in his life?

His best bet would be to go right on smudge-swatting, to adapt his style of play to the tennis court.

So how does he go about "smudge-swatting" on a tennis court? Simple: All he has to do is hit the Touchpoint on his Invisible Shield. You see, smudges and Touchpoints have one thing in common. They both represent the exact point the ball enters the Positive Contact Zone.

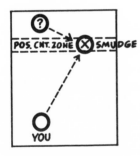 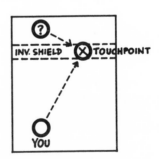

So whether he swats a smudge on his Plexiglas wall or hits a Touchpoint on his Invisible Shield, what he is really doing is contacting the ball at the exact point it enters his Positive Contact Zone.

Besides, when he hits the Touchpoint on his Invisible

Shield, not only does the ball bounce back, he also gets a
smudge in the middle of his strings.

Whacko! Movement → Countermovement → Contact (+).

Another smudge bites the dust.

4

Design A and Design B

<table>
<tr>
<td align="center">Design A
Watch the Ball/
Hit the Ball</td>
<td align="center">Design B
Look for the Touchpoint/
Hit the Touchpoint</td>
</tr>
<tr>
<td>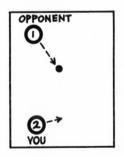</td>
<td>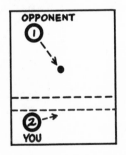</td>
</tr>
</table>

THESE TWO DIAGRAMS REPRESENT TWO DIFFERENT STYLES OF play, two entirely different "designs" for completing the contact sequence on a tennis court.

Design A and Design B.

In both designs *you* are in the position of countermovement, and your objective is to complete the contact sequence with Positive Contact.

Design A represents the traditional style of play; a design for completing the contact sequence that includes a basic set of directions:

1. Watch the ball.
2. Hit the ball.

Design B represents an alternate style of play that also includes a basic set of directions for completing the contact sequence:

1. Look for the Touchpoint on your Invisible Shield.
2. Hit the Touchpoint on your Invisible Shield.

The difference in these two designs is the difference between playing tennis and playing tennis "in the zone."

Design A: Watch the Ball/Hit the Ball

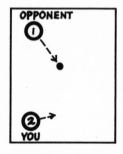

"Watching the ball," as we have seen, is a variable focus tracking pattern (V-Trak). In other words, a tracking pattern based on the ball—a variable.

But what about "hitting the ball"? What sort of pattern is that? It seems only logical that to complete the contact sequence the ball and your racket must come together at a contact point. This is true. In order to complete the contact sequence there must be a Contact Event between the ball and your racket, and the traditional pattern for producing this Contact Event is to hit the ball with your racket. Very logical. But just as "watching the ball" is a visual tracking pattern based on variable, so, too, "hitting the ball" is a "motor-intercept pattern" based on the same variable: the ball.

In other words, hit the ball is a "Variable Base Motor Intercept Pattern." "Motor-Ball" for short.

Put these two patterns together and you get the basic visual/motor patterns inherent to traditional tennis.

1. Watch the ball: a variable focus tracking pattern (V-Trak).

2. Hit the ball: a variable base intercept pattern (Motor-Ball).

Design A: V-Trak/Motor-Ball, the traditional design for completing the contact sequence. A design based on a variable—the ball.

Design B: Look for the Touchpoint/ Hit the Touchpoint

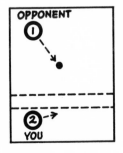

Design B involves an alteration in both the visual tracking pattern and the motor intercept pattern used to complete the contact sequence. By "looking for the Touchpoint on your Invisible Shield" you are changing your visual tracking pattern from a variable focus pattern (V-Trak) to a fixed focus pattern (F-Trak). And by "hitting the Touchpoint on your Invisible Shield" you are changing your motor intercept pattern from a variable base pattern (motor-ball) to a fixed base pattern. "Motor-Zone" for short.

In other words, instead of basing your countermovements on a physical variable — the ball, the idea in Motor-Zone is to base your countermovements on a physical constant — a fixed Positive Contact Zone.

Put these two patterns together and you get the basic visual/motor patterns inherent to Design B:

1. Look for the Touchpoint on your Invisible Shield: a fixed focus tracking pattern (F-Trak).

2. Hit the Touchpoint on your Invisible Shield: a fixed base motor intercept pattern (Motor-Zone).

Design B: F-Trak/Motor-Zone, an alternate design for completing the contact sequence. A design based on a constant — the contact zone.

Playing tennis "in the zone" is really quite easy, once you know the zone in which you are trying to play.

The Countermovement Continuum

In tennis, every countermovement you make is a combination of "technique" and "timing." Together, your technique and your timing form an important coexistence. You can't have one without the other. You can't have technique without timing, nor can you have timing without technique. They go together like space and time; a continuum.

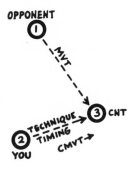

If you give this diagram some motion, you can see that the contact sequence is actually a relationship in space and time between movement and countermovement. In fact, every contact sequence in tennis involves this space/time relationship, and to create a positive Contact Event, your countermovements must form a positive relationship in space and time with the movement of the ball. In other words, not only must your countermovements relate in "space" to the movement of the ball, they must also relate in "time" to the movement of the ball.

How your countermovements relate in space to the movement of the ball is your "technique." How they relate in time to the movement of the ball is your "timing." Technique and timing—the countermovement continuum.

Positiming and Negatiming

Before I chanced onto this Invisible Shield idea, I had always taught the game of tennis in the traditional manner, which is to say I taught my students the proper "techniques" involved in hitting a tennis ball. I taught what we tennis pros like to call "sound fundamentals." This is how you take your racket back, this is how you move your feet, this is how you swing your racket forward. The linear, turn-step-swing approach to the game. And I was very good at it. You have to be good at it to become a member of the United States Professional Tennis Association.

But during all the years I spent teaching sound fundamentals, I never really thought I was getting to the heart of the matter. I was teaching my students the strokes, but I wasn't teaching them the game. Besides, how many ways can you tell someone to move his feet? After eighteen years it was driving me crazy!

But just about the time I was getting ready to bag the whole thing and start looking for a normal job, I chanced onto this crazy shield idea, and not only did it change my whole approach to playing the game of tennis, it also changed my whole approach to teaching the game of tennis.

This is not to say that I completely discounted the traditional approach to teaching. On the contrary, the linear approach has produced too many top-notch tennis players to be discounted. But just because it is the accepted norm for tennis instruction, does not mean it is the only way to teach the game. There are other ways of teaching that involve learning an overall concept of what is going on out there, rather than a breakdown of how to move your feet.

For instance, as a teaching tool, the Shield was extremely helpful in explaining a very tricky concept in tennis, the concept of timing. Or, more exactly, the difference between good timing (Positiming) and bad timing (Negatiming).

Here's what I mean:

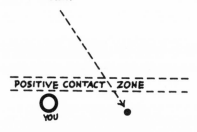

Give this ball some motion and you will see that it passes through the Positive Contact Zone in a certain amount of time. The amount of time the ball spends in the Positive Contact Zone is the positive contact time, and Positiming is when your racket contacts the ball *during* the Positive Contact time.

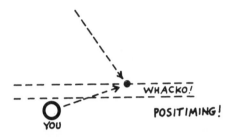

Negatiming, on the other hand, is when your racket contacts the ball *after* the Positive Contact time.

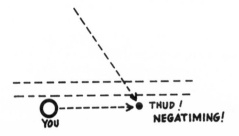

Whenever your countermovements are negatimed, your chances for Positive Contact are considerably reduced. Negatiming is a definite minus. It acts *against* the creation of a Positive Contact Event. Positiming is a plus. It acts *toward* the creation of a Positive Contact Event.

By using an Invisible Shield to pre-define your Positive Contact Zone it is easy to determine whether your timing is good or bad. Any time contact occurs *at* your Shield your timing was good. Any time contact occurs *behind* your Shield your timing was bad.

Motor-Ball Versus Motor-Zone

Design A
Hit the Ball

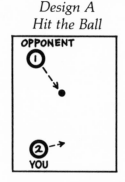

Design B
Hit the Touchpoint

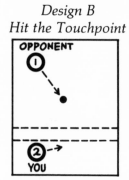

There is a distinct "physical" difference between "hitting the ball" (Motor-Ball) and "hitting the Touchpoint on your Invisible Shield" (Motor-Zone), that can best be seen by adding up what you get at the Contact Event.

In both cases, whether you hit the ball or whether you hit the Touchpoint on your Invisible Shield, you get a Contact Event containing the same three things:

1.   One object of movement – ball.
2.   One object of countermovement – racket.
3.   One Contact Point – location.

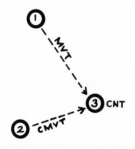

This means the end result of Motor-Ball and Motor-Zone is the same: a Contact Event between the ball and your racket. The big difference between hitting the ball and hitting the Touchpoint lies in the actual "location" of the Contact Event. In other words, when you hit the ball you get a Contact Event located somewhere along the flight line of the ball, but when you hit the Touchpoint on your Invisible Shield you get a Contact Event located at the exact point the ball enters your Positive Contact Zone. And contact at the exact *point* the ball enters your Positive Contact Zone is also contact at the exact *time* the ball enters your Positive Contact Zone—and that spells Positiming.

What does this mean? It means that every time you hit the ball you'll get a Contact Event between the ball and your racket, and if you time your stroke correctly you will always make contact in your Positive Contact Zone. That is, *if* you time your stroke correctly, and as we all know, good timing takes a long time to develop, right?

Wrong. With Motor-Zone, every time you hit the Touchpoint on your Invisible Shield you will not only get a Contact Event, you will also get the bonus of a Contact Event in your Positive Contact Zone—every time. And that's a nice bonus when you think about it—Automatic Positiming.

That's the difference between Motor-Ball and Motor-Zone. With Motor-Ball good timing must be developed. With Motor-Zone good timing is inherent to the motor intercept pattern itself. Every time you hit the Touchpoint on your Invisible Shield you get a Contact Event that was positimed. You might say Motor-Zone includes Positiming in its overall design. Motor-Ball does not.

So why not simply hit the *ball* at the exact point it enters your Positive Contact Zone? That would certainly solve the problems you have with bad timing. Which is true. If you could contact every ball at the exact point it enters your Positive Contact Zone, then you would have very good timing. Except there is a problem with the basics of Design A. In order to hit the ball, you must first watch the ball. But while you are watching the ball, how do you know where your Positive Contact Zone is? What are you doing to mark the location of your Positive Contact Zone? With your eyes focused on the ball you know one thing for certain: They are *not* focused on your contact zone. So how do you know the location of your Positive Contact Zone? That's the problem with watching the ball. You might know where the ball is, but you don't know where your contact zone is. So how can you tell exactly where and when the ball enters your Positive Contact Zone?

When you look for the Touchpoint on your Invisible Shield, you definitely know the location of your Positive Contact Zone. Your eyes are focused on it. As to knowing where the ball is, that's easy. It's the fuzzy yellow thing coming into focus, and you can tell exactly where and when the ball enters your Positive Contact Zone because that's when the ball is visually the clearest.

It's a crazy turn-around on everything I ever learned about playing and teaching the game of tennis. The craziest thing of all is that it works.

5

The Cognitive Pattern

THE MORE I STARTED USING THIS SHIELD IDEA IN MY OWN game, the more I started wondering about the strange sensation that accompanied the whole process. What was going on? Why did it feel so weird, yet work so well? I was beginning to see that F-Trak, as a visual tracking pattern, was more efficient than V-Trak, because it eliminated the problem of refocusing during the contact sequence. I was also beginning to see that Motor-Zone, as a motor intercept pattern, was more efficient than Motor-Ball because it included Positiming, where Motor-Ball did not.

And it's not like I didn't try both ways. In fact, as I got better at Design B, I also found that I got better at Design A.

What I would do is try playing tennis one way, then try it the other. For one set, I would use Design A, and since Design A was the design I grew up with, I was already pretty good at it. Two decades of watch the ball/hit the ball and you get pretty good at it.

Then, for the next set, I would use Design B. In other words, instead of playing a whole set in which I watched the ball/hit the ball, I switched, and tried playing a whole set where I looked for the Touchpoint/hit the Touchpoint.

It was like a big experiment, using myself as the guinea pig. And because I went at it as an experiment, it was a lot easier to deal with the strange sensation that always accompanied visualizing a Shield across my contact zone. What was this hypnotic sensation? It was almost as if I was meditating on "something" that was really "nothing." This crazy Invisible Shield had more to it than I had ever imagined. But as strange as it was at first, it was still logical. By visualizing a Shield across my contact zone, I always had a visual reference for exactly where and when I should contact the ball. In fact, it was a reference for contacting every ball. It made sense, actually. I just couldn't believe it worked! I mean, a visual tracking pattern where you don't watch the ball, and a motor intertcept pattern where you don't hit the ball. What kind of logic is that? It *sounded* so wrong, yet it kept on working. So I kept on trying to figure it out. And sooner or later it all had to lead to the brain. After all, in any sport involving eye-hand coordination, the organ responsible for all that coordinating is your brain, and just as Design B uses an "altered" visual tracking pattern to input information to the brain, it also uses an "altered" cognitive processing pattern to process that information. In other words, by visualizing a Shield across your contact zone, not only do you alter your tracking pattern, you simultaneously alter your state of consciousness.

That's what playing tennis "in the zone" is all about — playing tennis in an altered state of consciousness, a state of consciousness different from your normal conscious state. That's what felt so strange. Every time I switched from watching the ball to visualizing a Shield across my contact zone, I was simultaneously switching from my normal state of consciousness to an altered state. And, more importantly, the more I practiced making the switch to this altered conscious state, the more comfortable I became with it. I found it wasn't anything weird at all, although the overall sensation was one of playing tennis in a daydream. And when I thought about it, that's exactly what I was doing. Only instead of the daydream being *inside* my mind's eye, it was a daydream taking place right out there on the tennis court, and I was a part of it. The funny thing is, my daydream game was more efficient than my normal game. The visual tracking pattern was more efficient. The motor intercept pattern was more efficient. It made me wonder if perhaps the cognitive processing pattern might also be more efficient. Was playing tennis in a daydream actually more efficient than playing tennis in my normal conscious state?

Ha! "Daydream Tennis," I thought to myself. That ought to go over real big in a world where "sound biomechanical technique" is the name of the game. How do you go about telling your students that daydreaming while you play tennis is actually sound cognitive technique? I felt like I was bucking some immense system, and sometimes the whole thing sounded too crazy, too strange to explain.

Everything about Design B went counter to the traditional way I had learned to play the game. In fact, Design B went *so* counter to the traditional style of play, that it began to show some logic. For instance: Where Design A has certain inherent rules for what to do with your eyes (watch the ball), and what to do with your body (hit the ball), it also has an inherent rule for what to do with your mind (concentrate on the ball).

All in all, Design A is a very logical design for playing the game of tennis. A design whose visual/cognitive/motor patterns are all based on a common object — the ball. That's what makes it logical. The whole design is based on *one* thing—the ball. Unfortunately, the ball is a variable, which makes Design A a "Variable-Base Design" for countermovement.

Design B also has certain inherent rules for what to do with your eyes (look for the Touchpoint on your Invisible Shield), and what to do with your body (hit the Touchpoint on your Invisible Shield), but the most interesting part of Design B is the part on what to do with your mind (concentrate on your Invisible Shield).

As I was starting to find out, even though Design B *sounded* completely backwards, there was a definite logic to the overall design.

Like Design A, Design B is a design in which visual, cognitive, and motor patterns are all based on a common object—your Invisible Shield, meaning the whole design is based on *one* thing—a fixed Positive Contact Zone. A constant. Which makes Design B a "Fixed-Base" design for countermovement.

The more I tried out both designs, the more I found out about the difference in what I was doing with my mind when I concentrated on the ball, and what I was doing with my mind when I concentrated on my Invisible Shield. It was the difference between using half my brain to solve the problem of Positive Contact, and using my whole brain to solve the same problem.

Half-Brain Versus Whole-Brain

The human brain is divided into two hemispheres that continually interact with each other in different patterns.

These different "cognitive patterns" are accompanied by different states of consciousness. For instance, when you play tennis in your normal state of consciousness, your brain is operating in an "asymmetrical" cognitive pattern. Which means one hemisphere of your brain is handling most of the mental processing while the other hemisphere is contributing in a subordinate manner.

So when you play tennis in your normal state of consciousness you are essentially solving the problem of Positive Contact with only half your brain. Of course, when you look at all the highly competent tennis players who play the game in their normal state of consciousness, it becomes obvious that the problem of Positive Contact *can* be solved by engaging only one hemisphere of the brain. That's not the point. The point is, if you can solve the problem of Positive Contact by using only half your brain, imagine how much better you could solve the problem of Positive Contact if you switched on the whole thing?

Question: How do you switch on your whole brain and play tennis at the same time?

Answer: Give *both* hemispheres of your brain something to work with. After all, if you want your whole brain to start working for you on the tennis court you must first activate both sides, get both hemispheres involved in the task at hand. In other words, if you want to play whole brain tennis, you have to challenge your whole brain.

That's what playing tennis "in the zone" is really all about. Playing tennis with your "whole brain." Switching from an asymmetrical pattern in which one hemisphere of your brain dominates the cognitive process, to a "symmetrical" pattern in which *both* hemispheres of your brain are engaged simultaneously.

The trick, of course, is being able to make the switch from half brain to whole brain. Just how does one go about activating the left and right hemispheres of the brain simultaneously?

When you think about it, the dominant hemisphere (generally, the left hemisphere) is already activated when you walk onto the court to play tennis. The act of walking onto the court to play tennis is enough of a task to activate the left hemisphere of your brain. *That's* not the problem. The problem is the right hemisphere, the subordinate hemisphere. How do you bring the right hemisphere out of its subordinate role and get it involved in solving the problem of Positive Contact? How do you activate the hemisphere most closely associated with visualization, imagination, seeing with the mind's eye?

One way is to actively *use* your imagination while you are playing tennis, to literally "activate" your powers of visualization right out there on the tennis court.

That's where the Invisible Shield comes in. By visualizing an imaginary Shield across your contact zone, not only are you activating the right hemisphere of your brain, you are also using your powers of visualization in a directed, meaningful way: to perpetually reference the location of your Positive Contact Zone.

The more I kept working with Design B, the more I started to realize how well this mystery fit together. By visualizing a Shield across my contact zone, not only was I switching on my whole brain, I was also fixing my focus on my contact zone, which is the essence of a fixed focus tracking pattern, which is the essence of Design B. Good old F-Trak.

Was F-Trak really the secret to switching from playing half-brain tennis to playing whole-brain tennis?

If it was, then what I had happened onto accidentally might prove helpful to other tennis players as well. After all, even though we all play the game at different levels, using different styles and different strokes, we all have something in common. Something that brings us all together as tennis players. We all have brains, and we all have to use our brains to solve the same problem — the problem of Positive Contact. It doesn't matter if you are a little kid just taking up the game, or a super senior competing in your last national championships. It doesn't matter if you play on the crack-filled courts down at City Park or Center Court at Wimbledon. It doesn't matter if you use a brand new, oversized graphite racket, or an old, beat-up Kramer. The name of the game is the same for all of us: We make Positive Contact or we lose.

That's quite a challenge when you think about it, and your brain loves a challenge. The problem is, *you* are the only one who can challenge your own brain. Which is what it takes to play tennis "in the zone." You have to challenge your whole brain, and when you challenge your whole brain, the strangest thing happens. It accepts the challenge for as long as you challenge it. And when your whole brain takes on the problem of Positive Contact, you get a chance to see the "whole-you" in action, the whole-you solving the problem of Positive Contact on a tennis court.

It's quite an exhilarating experience, a total synchrony of eyes, mind, and body. The whole-you at one with the game of tennis. All it takes is a little imagination mixed into the reality of the contact sequence. It's really very easy to switch on your whole brain, but the switch from a pattern of cognitive asymmetry to a pattern of cognitive symmetry brings with it a switch in your state of consciousness. And this change in conscious states feels very strange at first. Like you are daydreaming and playing tennis at the same time.

When I first started using on-court visualization in my own game, I found this daydream sensation disconcerting at times. Like most tennis players, I grew up under traditional tennis dogma, the dogma that says watch the ball/hit the ball/NO DAYDREAMING ALLOWED! The thought of concentrating on anything other than the ball was strictly taboo. One simply did *not* daydream while one was playing tennis.

Yet the more I investigated playing tennis in this altered, symmetrical state, the more I realized I was bringing out a part of me I had always inhibited on the court. And it was a part of me that I liked, a part of me that didn't hold back on the tennis court. What was it about concentrating on my Positive Contact Zone that brought out this hidden me? It made me wonder if there was something hidden in what I was concentrating on, something substantial, something logical that might help explain the strange sensation of zoning. Was there something more to the contact zone than just the contact zone?

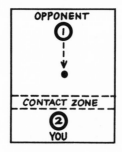

The answer was right in front of my eyes.

6

Future-Focus

Diagram A

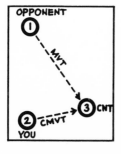

Diagram B

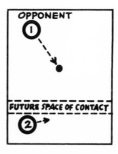

DIAGRAM A DEPICTS A COMPLETE CONTACT SEQUENCE FROM beginning to end. It begins with the movement of the ball, followed by your countermovements, ending with contact.

MVT ➔ CMVT ➔ CNT

1 ➔ 2 ➔ 3

Diagram B depicts the same contact sequence, only in Diagram B the contact sequence is incomplete. There is movement; there is countermovement, but the Contact Event has yet to occur. Point 3 hasn't happened yet. It is a point that lies somewhere in the future of the contact sequence. A "future-point" that is simultaneously the future-point of movement, the future-point of countermovement, and the future-point of contact. That makes three future-points all rolled up into one future-point, the Touchpoint on your Invisible Shield, which gives the surface of your Invisible Shield a very definitive reference in the linear time scheme of every contact sequence. Your Invisible Shield is the "Future Space of Contact," and when you visualize a Shield across your contact zone, you are literally fixing your focus on your own future.

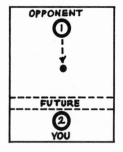

That's what was hidden away in this crazy puzzle—a logical reason for visualizing a shield across your contact zone. It fixes your focus on the future of the contact sequence. I started calling it "Future-Focus" because that's the name that best describes what you are really doing when you focus on your contact zone. You are focusing on your future.

It made sense, and it helped explain another piece of the puzzle. The piece that says: If focusing on your contact zone is future-focus, then what are you focusing on when you focus on the ball?

The Contact Point

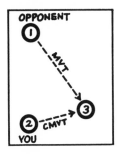

If you look at a typical contact sequence you can see that the Movement Event has a beginning point in time (Point 1) as well as an end point in time (Point 3). It is a complete occurrence from start to finish. Likewise, the Countermovement Event is a complete occurrence from start to finish. It has a beginning point in time (Point 2), and it has an end point in time (Point 3). And, if you look closely, you can see that the Contact Event is also a complete occurrence from beginning to end, only in the Contact Event the beginning point in time and the end point in time are very close together. They have measured it down to milliseconds. Can you imagine that? The whole object of the game of tennis taking place in a matter of milliseconds. And during that short amount of time you either create a Positive Contact Event or a Negative Contact Event.

Point 3 — the Contact Point. It is by far the most important point in the time and space of the contact sequence. Everything comes together at Point 3, and as it all comes together, Point 3 comes alive in all its paradox.

The Contact Point. It is at once an end point for one contact sequence while at the same time it is the beginning point for the next contact sequence.

The Contact Point — an end point and a beginning point, simultaneously. The point where it all comes together in space, and *when* it all comes together in time.

Past-Focus

Every contact sequence in the game of tennis moves through time as well as space, and this movement through time takes place in a logical order. In other words, every contact sequence has a Past, a Present, and a Future.

MVT →CMVT →CNT
1 →2 →3
Past →Present →Future

First comes the movement of the ball, beginning the contact sequence in time, laying down a logical past on which to base the countermovements you make in the present. Finally comes contact, a logical future for the contact sequence.

The problem that arises when you focus on the ball is that you are focusing on the event that *precedes* your countermovements in the present. In other words, when you focus on the ball you are focusing on the past event of the contact sequence. That's "Past-Focus," and that's the biggest problem with Design A. Everything about Design A is based on the movement of the ball.

1.   Watch the ball.
2.   Concentrate on the ball.

3.   Hit the ball.

When you add that up, you get an overall design for countermovement whose visual, cognitive, and motor patterns are all based on the past. Past-focus; it all starts with the focus of your eyes.

What I kept finding out through practicing both focusing patterns was that they both worked. I could watch the ball and play tennis in past-focus, or I could look for the Touchpoint on my Invisible Shield and play tennis in future-focus.

Past-focus and future-focus. They both work, but only one of them activates your whole brain.

7

The Challenge
of Zoning

ZONING IS NOT NEW. IN FACT, IT IS VERY OLD. IT GOES BY A
lot of names: concentration, visualization, meditation,
hypnosis, altered states, prayer. Whatever you call it, zoning deals with the mind. It is a mystery. It exists, but
nobody knows what it is. People have heard of it, tennis
players have experienced it, but it eludes explanation. It
hides in the wings, waiting to swoop in on you when you
least expect it. But it *does* happen. Tennis players have
known about it for years, athletes in every sport have experienced "the zone"; that mysterious, inexplicable sensation you get when, for no apparent reason, something
comes over you, something different, something special.
The result is a transcendence from the ordinary, an awareness of the game unlike any other. It is an experience of being one with the game, one with yourself. It is synchrony,
simultaneity, it is a dance between movement and countermovement choreographed in space and time by the human

brain — the whole brain, working in its most efficient operative state — the state of symmetry.

As systems of countermovement, we are symmetrical. We have a symmetrical visual input system (our eyes), connected to a symmetrical cognitive processing system (our brains), connected to a symmetrical motor output system (our bodies). Logically, the most efficient mode of operation for a symmetrical system is symmetrical, and that's what Design B is all about, symmetry. Putting yourself into a symmetrical mode of opertion, and playing tennis at the same time.

But with this symmetrical mode of operation comes a symmetrical state of consciousness, the conscious state you get when both hemispheres of your brain are actively engaged in the cognitive process. This whole-brain state is different than your ordinary state. You can feel it, sense it, you know it is happening when it happens. It takes hold of you, and what you experience is that special "oneness" with the game that has been around since the beginning of time.

All it takes is a simple change in the focus of your eyes, and that change in focus can cause an immediate change in the efficiency of your game. The choice is strictly yours. They are your eyes, and how you use them on the tennis court is completely up to you. You can focus on the ball, in which case you will be in past-focus, or you can focus on the contact zone, in which case you will be in future-focus.

Both focusing patterns work, but only you can decide if you want to focus on the past or on the future. Personally, future-focus felt very strange to me at first. Everything seemed turned around, backwards, and the feeling of daydreaming while I played tennis took a little getting used to. But the biggest challenge was not learning how to play tennis in the zone myself, it was learning how to teach it to others.

How does one go about teaching whole-brain tennis?

You don't just walk up to someone and say: "Hey! Wanna learn how to use your whole brain out there on the court?"

People think you're nuts. Especially when the thrust of modern day teaching is "sound biomechanical technique." That's the way I learned to play the game, and that's the way I learned to teach the game. But all along I felt there was something missing. Something wasn't right. Sound biomechanical technique was all fine and dandy, but learning how to swing your racket isn't all that hard. In fact, the basic countermovements in tennis are easy to teach and easy to learn. So why do people have so much trouble playing the game? Could there be something inherently difficult with the fundamental approach of watch the ball/hit the ball? In a game that perpetually flows toward the future, focusing on the past is backwards, and watch the ball/hit the ball is past-focus. Design A is based on past-focus, but Design A is accepted, tried and true. Watch the ball/hit the ball has been around for a long time, and it always will be around. Past-focus is not only a pattern we use to play our games, it is also a pattern we use to live our lives. So is future-focus, only future-focus is a bit more subtle, more challenging to the mind than past-focus. In life, future-focus has a lot to do with planning ahead, visualizing goals, looking to the future. On a tennis court it works the same way:

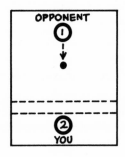

When you visualize a shield across your contact zone you are planning ahead, defining the contact zone with the focus of your eyes. You are literally looking to the future of the contact sequence — the contact zone. Within its boundaries exist the future space of movement, the future space of countermovement, and the future space of contact. Three futures in one future. If you want to plan ahead, the contact zone is the logical place to start, and if you want to play tennis "in the zone" the contact zone is also the logical place to start. After all, that's where it all comes together.

Getting to Know Your Contact Zone

One of the benefits of teaching people how to play tennis in the zone is that I am really teaching higher consciousness on the tennis court. It's exciting. I get a chance to deal with people who are learning how to open up their minds, people who are discovering their own potential, both mentally and physically.

For some people this is a completely new experience, for others it is something they always knew they had deep down inside, and Design B gives them a way to bring it out into the open.

But Design B is a challenge. It requires a willingness to deal with the subject of concentration. A symmetrical state is highly concentrative, absolutely focused in space and time. But don't let that scare you away. Just because something is a challenge doesn't mean it can't be achieved. Engaging the whole brain in the problem of Positive Contact is definitely within the capabilities of the human species. Our brains would not have evolved into symmetrical structures if they weren't meant to be used symmetrically.

The challenge you will have to face head-on (no pun) is

the challenge of switching from your normal state of consciousness to an altered, symmetrical state. Some people
take to symmetry like a fish takes to water. Some people
don't like it at all. Even if it works! The point is, it works!
Your brain is an amazingly accurate instrument when you
tune in the whole thing. But when you tune in your whole
brain you will also get the strange sensation that comes
with it. Of course, you also get a lot more Positive Contact
due to the symmetrical input/processing/output mode you
are in.

It's a paradoxical trade-off—feels strange/works great.
Whole-brain tennis—all it takes is a little imagination
superimposed on the reality of the contact sequence.

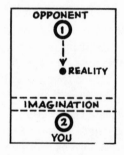

Care to challenge your mind?

8

Playing Tennis in the Zone

Defending Your Shield

How does one go about learning to play tennis in the zone? The most direct way is to start by learning what it feels like to visualize a Shield across your contact zone. Here's an easy game to get you started. If you can't find a willing practice partner, you can always find a willing wall.

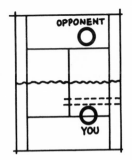 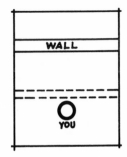

DESIGN B

Stand at the service line as seen in the diagram above, or about 15 to 20 feet from the wall, and visualize an an imaginary Shield located arm's-length in front of you. This Invisible Shield rises from the surface of the court to the highest point you can reach your racket, and spans half the width of the court, from the center line of the outside doubles line.

This is a "half-shield," and the name of the game is "Defend your Invisible Shield." Your objective is simple — don't let the ball get past your Invisible Shield.

That's all. Simple game, simple objective. Every time your opponent hits the ball toward your Invisible Shield, take the flat side of your trusty tennis racket and see if you can keep the ball from penetrating your shield.

Helpful hint: When you first go at this game, don't worry about your form. The object is to make sure nothing gets past your Invisible Shield. Use whatever form it takes. Improvise if you have to, go free form, but defend your Invisible Shield for as long as you possibly can.

Remember, in this game, you are not trying to beat your opponent. Rather, the object is to visualize an imaginary barrier across your contact zone and defend it with your racket. Nothing gets past your Invisible Shield.

You will find that defending your Invisible Shield is a highly competitive game, involving movement, counter-movement, and contact, just like the highly competitive game of tennis. Only there is something about the game of defending your Invisible Shield that makes it slightly different from the normal game of tennis. It is a game that requires the active use of your imagination. After all, you can't defend your Invisible Shield unless you have an Invisible Shield to defend, and the only way to get an Invisible Shield is to create it with your own mind. You have to visualize it, and when you visualize a Shield across your contact zone you create a situation that simultaneously engages both hemispheres of your brain in a symmetrical processing pattern.

Bingo! That's when you make the switch from half-brain to whole-brain. It is also when you get the strange sensation of playing tennis and daydreaming at the same time. But that's what defending your Invisible Shield is all about. It is at once a very *real* game of movement/countermovement/contact. It is also a daydream.

Bring the two together, and you have the essence of playing tennis "in the zone."

A Test of Your Timing

The imaginary game of defending your Invisible Shield has a way of telling it like it is. In other words, as you go about making countermovements to defend your Shield from the movement of the ball, you will get a very honest appraisal of your own timing in every contact sequence. If contact occurred *behind* your Shield, then your countermovements for that particular contact sequence were negatimed. This does not mean you will produce Negative Contact. It just means that your countermovements formed a negative relationship in time with the movement of the ball, which lowers your odds for Positive Contact.

If, however, contact occurred *at* your Invisible Shield, then your countermovements for that particular contact sequence were positimed. This does not mean you will always produce Positive Contact, but if your countermovements form a positive relationship in time with the movement of the ball, you will certainly raise your odds.

Contact *at* your Shield—Positiming.

Contact *behind* your Shield—Negatiming.

Think of this game as a self-evaluation of your own timing. A countermovement, remember, is a combination of technique and timing:

$$\frac{\text{Technique}}{\text{Timing}} = \text{Countermovement}$$

Defending your Invisible Shield is a game that will show you, firsthand, just how well your countermovements relate in time to the movement of the ball. Don't be discouraged if you find a lot of contact occurring behind your Shield. At first, Negatiming is a common problem. It pervades the game. We have all shared the feeling of being late for contact. Everybody who plays the game of tennis knows what it is like to be "off" on your timing. But how do you fix the problem? How do you turn your timing on?

One way is to turn on your whole brain. In a symmetrical state, positiming is easy. It comes with the territory.

The Contact Quadrants

Once you get the hang of defending your Invisible Shield, it is time to start expanding your awareness of your contact zone.

If you can visualize a Shield across your contact zone, you can also visualize a Shield divided into four quadrants. As you look at it, it looks like this.

HIGH LEFT	HIGH RIGHT
LOW LEFT	LOW RIGHT

These are your Contact Quadrants. Every ball that is hit in your direction will enter your contact zone in one of these quadrants: High Left, Low Left, High Right, Low Right. If you are righthanded, any ball that enters the high right quadrant is a high forehand, while any ball entering your low right quadrant is a low forehand. High left is a high backhand, low left is a low backhand. For lefthanders, everything is the opposite.

These Contact Quadrants are very useful in evaluating the strengths and weaknesses of your game. For instance, you might contact every ball that enters the right side of your contact zone *at* or very near your Invisible Shield. Whacko! That's a strength. But you might also contact every ball that enters the left side of your contact zone *behind* your Invisible Shield. Thud! That's a weakness.

The reason is apparent when you look at your strokes from the perspective of your contact zone. Whenever the ball enters the right side of your contact zone your timing is good, but whenever the ball enters the left side of your contact zone your timing is bad.

This pattern of Positiming on one side of your contact zone and Negatiming on the other side of your contact zone is a very common pattern in tennis, particularly at the beginning and intermediate levels. It is a pattern of variable timing.

How many times have you seen a player with a good forehand and a bad backhand? It is a common tennis phenomenon. The "B League Syndrome." It strikes us all at one time or another, but it is a problem that can be solved by simply changing your timing pattern from a variable to a constant. That's what happens when you contact every ball *at* your Invisible Shield. You change your timing pattern from a variable to a constant, the constant of Positiming. It is a constant that can pull your game together in a hurry, but it is a constant that takes concentration. Remember, you can't contact the ball at your Invisible Shield unless you first create an Invisible Shield, and that takes concentration — whole-brain concentration, the most efficient kind.

Linear Madness

Have you ever felt there is too much to think about in tennis, and not enough time to think about it? It's an age-old problem in sport and an age-old problem in the teaching of sport. There you are, standing on the court, wondering which stroke to use for which ball, which grip to use for which stroke, which foot do you step on, which knee do you bend, should you swivel your hips, rotate your shoulders, stand on your head, twiddle your thumbs, what the heck is going on out here? There is absolutely no way you can think about everything you have to think about in the amount of time you have to think about it.

It can drive you crazy! Linear madness. I see it all the time on the courts. It goes something like this: The traditional way of teaching and learning the game is through a series of linear steps. First you do this, then you do this, and then you do this, and what you end up with is the perfect linear stroke. Thank you very much, that'll be ten dollars, please.

Sorry folks, but it doesn't really happen that way on the court, even though you *can* learn to play the game through a series of linear steps. In fact, the history of teaching tennis is a history of breaking the game down into its basic linear segments. The theory being, the more you break something down into its component parts, the more you know about how it works. Sound biomechanics — the basic turn/step/swing approach. It's all very neat. It's all very understandable. It's all very linear. It does, however, fall a little short in one category. You see, breaking something down into its linear parts is not the same as putting it back together as a linear whole.

> Humpty Dumpty sat on a wall,
> Humpty Dumpty had a great fall,
> All the King's biomechanics experts,
> Took slow motion films of the tragedy,
> Analyzed it, linearized it,
> Showed Humpty his problem—
> Mounted up, and went home to Pac-Man.

Humpty, unfortunately, was left the tedious task of putting himself back together again.

Moral: You can break it down till there is nothing left but pieces, but the name of the game is putting the pieces together, and that's what Design B is all about—putting the pieces of your game together into a linear whole.

9
Expanding Your Zone

The Full-Shield

WHEN I TEACH PEOPLE HOW TO PLAY TENNIS IN THE ZONE, we generally start at the service line with a half-shield, then move to the "T" and expand to a "full-shield."

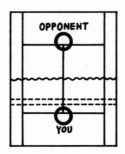

A full-shield gives you more area to cover and involves an expanded awareness of your peripheries. This takes time to develop, but with practice you will soon find that it is possible to visually encompass the entire width of your contact zone from one sideline to the other.

Whether you are using a half-shield or a full-shield, the object of your imaginary game remains the same: Contact every ball *at* your Shield, whether it be a floater into the high right quadrant, a line drive into the low left quadrant, off the bounce, in the air, it doesn't matter. Once you have fixed the location of your full-shield, make sure nothing gets past it.

Contact *at* your Shield—Positiming.

Contact *behind* your Shield—Negatiming.

Controlling Your Contact Zone

As you expand the *width* of your contact zone by visualizing a full-shield, you can also play a game that will help you expand your awareness of the *depth* of your contact zone. It's called "name your depth," and it goes like this:

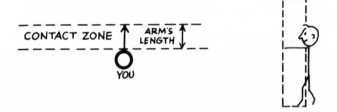

Imagine your contact zone is an area of space that has depth as well as height and width. The "depth" of your contact zone extends from arm's-length in front of you, back to your body.

Here's a closer look:

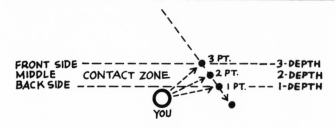

The front side of your contact zone is located arm's-length in front of you — that's a 3-depth. The back side of your contact zone is at your body — that's a 1-depth. The exact middle of your contact zone is a 2-depth.

Every time your opponent hits a ball toward your contact zone, a competition begins. It is a competition for control of the contact zone.

As the ball passes through your contact zone, you can conceivably make contact at a 3-depth, a 2-depth, or a 1-depth. If you make contact at a 3, then you have contacted the ball at the exact moment it enters your contact zone, which means the movement of the ball has not penetrated your contact zone. So in that particular contact sequence *you*, as countermovement, were in control of your contact zone. And when you are in control of your contact zone, the end result is usually Positive Contact.

In the next contact sequence, however, you make contact at a 1-depth. In this case, the movement of the ball has penetrated the full depth of your contact zone, which means movement controlled the contact zone in that particular contact sequence. And when movement controls the contact zone, the end result is usually Negative Contact.

But what about making contact right square in the middle of your contact zone? The 2-depth. The 2-depth sounds, at first, like the perfect depth of contact. But when you think about it, contact at a 2-depth means the movement of the ball has penetrated your contact zone by half its depth.

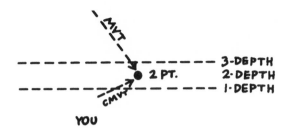

Contact at a 2-depth is 50/50 contact; the most deceiving kind. The movement of the ball controls the front half of your contact zone, while you control the back half. Half and half. Sometimes you get Positive Contact, sometimes you get Negative Contact. Contact at a 2-depth, however, is better than contact at a 1-depth. At least, when you make contact at a 2-depth, you know you are in control of the back half of your contact zone. But have you ever wondered what it would be like to be in control of the front half of your contact zone?

It is a question you can start to answer by seeing for yourself just how well you control your contact zone. As you hit the ball back and forth from the service line, start naming your depth of contact. Did contact occur at a 3-depth, a 2-depth, or a 1-depth?

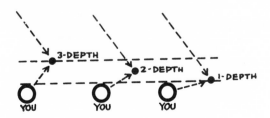

This is another one of those games that tells it like it is. When you contact the ball with your racket, contact usually occurs at one of these three depths.

When contact occurs at a 3-depth, *you* control the contact zone.

When contact occurs at a 2-depth, it's 50/50.

When contact occurs at a 1-depth the *ball* controls the contact zone.

Give your overall game a test by seeing how well your countermovements relate to your contact zone. You might be surprised at what you find out. Just say 3, 2, or 1 when you know the answer. And remember, the object of this game is not to beat your opponent, nor is it to win the point. The object of this game is to be "objective" about your *own* game. It doesn't matter if you are an absolute beginner or a touring pro. When you go onto the court, your contact zone goes with you, and how your countermovements relate to your contact zone is how your countermovements relate to the future of every contact sequence.

How do *your* countermovements relate to the future?

It is a challenging question. Focus on your contact zone, and you will "see" some honest answers.

10

Your Full Potential

LEARNING TO PLAY TENNIS IN THE ZONE IS LIKE LEARNING ANY-thing else. It takes time, it takes practice, but mostly it takes an unusual kind of courage. The courage to let go, to jump from the safety of your normal state of consciousness into the mysteries of a symmetrical state. The courage to be one with yourself.

It's exciting to know that every time you walk onto the court you have the ability to put yourself into a state of consciousness free of inhibition, free of doubt, free of the fear of losing. And all it takes is a small adjustment in your operating procedure, a change in your focus. It is a minor change that pays major dividends.

Changing from past-focus to future-focus is easy in theory. All you have to do is stop focusing on the space and time of the ball, and start focusing on the space and time of the contact zone.

In reality, future-focus takes practice. You don't learn to

control your focus overnight. When I first started experimenting with F-Trak, I found it difficult to control my focus. My eyes would wander all over the court, but the more I practiced controlling my focus, fixing it on my contact zone, the more I found out about the efficiency of a fixed-focus tracking pattern compared to a variable focus tracking pattern. And when you grow up playing watch the ball/hit the ball, teaching watch the ball/hit the ball, eating, sleeping, breathing watch the ball/hit the ball, it comes as quite a surprise to learn that all along you didn't have to watch the ball/hit the ball. There is another way, a more efficient way to use your eyes, your brain, and your body in a movement/countermovement confrontation. And the whole design is put into action by simply switching from V-Trak to F-Trak. That's where the switch from a half-brain pattern to a whole-brain pattern takes place, and it all happens simultaneously, everything kicks in at once. It's like switching yourself on. And the best thing is, you don't have to be an ace tennis player to do it. Anyone can learn to play tennis in the zone. It's not something that sneaks up on you in the dark. Nor does it happen only to those players who have mastered the "techniques" of the game. On the contrary, zoning is a state of mind, a concentrative state you produce yourself. And nowhere in the rules does it say you have to be a Wimbledon prospect to use the inherent capabilities of your own mind.

What you *do* have to be is willing; willing to let go of the past and switch your focus to the future. That takes courage. It is the courage to go to a different place in time, to step beyond the traditional boundaries of past-focus and look into the future. It's easy on a tennis court. Your future is right in front of you. The question is, can you focus on it? You see, in order to focus on your contact zone you must *not* focus on the ball. And that takes concentration.

F-Trak Feedback

For most players future-focus is a new experience on the tennis court, an experience in change — radical change. This experience can be exciting, disturbing, mind-boggling, but it is always a challenge. You see, Design B is meant to bring out your full potential on the tennis court. And if you have never seen yourself playing the game to your full potential, you are in for a treat.

So what's the big challenge? It's the challenge of your full potential; a challenge that cannot be met while one hemisphere of your brain dominates the cognitive process. In other words, the challenge of your full potential is the challenge of your own mind. That's a pretty heavy challenge when you think about it.

Fortunately, you have options. You can opt to pass, in which case you will never know what you are missing, or you can opt to play, take the challenge, in which case you will open new channels into your own mystery.

It's all very strange when viewed in the context of traditional tennis. But all the stuff you hear about being "one with the game," all that stuff about harmony and synchrony, is no joke. It really exists, and it's there for the taking. All you have to do is look in the right place. Of course, when you look in the right place, it seems like you're looking in the wrong place. Which puts us right back where we started. Playing tennis in the zone is strange, radically different, a completely individual experience. And it's a freebie. All it takes is an honest try. For instance: When I first started experimenting with F-Trak, looking for the Touchpoint on my Invisible Shield, I found it difficult to control my focus. It was hard to keep my focus fixed on my contact zone, especially when I moved from the midcourt area into the backcourt area.

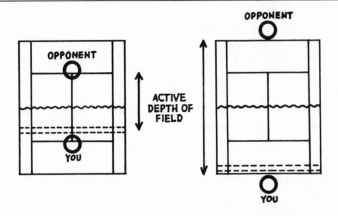

The "active depth of field" is considerably increased when you start hitting from baseline to baseline, and as I increased this depth I found it more difficult to keep my focus on my contact zone. But I kept at it, and I found that controlling my focus got easier the more I practiced controlling it. And as I got better at controlling my focus I got better at using F-Trak wherever I was on the court — forecourt, mid-court, or backcourt. I even started playing a visual game to observe the effects of F-Trak on my overall game. I called it "F-Trak Feedback," and to play it all I did was set a simple objective: Wherever I was located on the tennis court — forecourt, mid-court, or backcourt — I was going to use F-Trak regardless of the outcome. I was going to concentrate on performing a predefined visual tracking maneuver to the best of my ability — and simply observe what happened. I was curious to see whether a change in my signal sending procedure could truly make a difference in my whole-court game.

So I started looking for the Touchpoint on my Invisible Shield no matter where I was on the court. And to' give myself some instant feedback on how well I was doing, I started saying "yes" when I tracked the Touchpoint on my Invisible Shield, and "no" when I didn't.

F-Trak Feedback: "Yes" or "No" on tracking the Touch-point. It turned out to be an interesting game. I found that as I played it, not only did I get better at it, I also sensed myself going deeper into the zone. It was like another level of consciousness said: "Hey, you're pretty zoned out here, pal. But stick with it. You're heading in the right direction."

Actually, it didn't really say that, but I sensed the drift, you know? And the reason I knew I was heading in the right direction was that F-Trak kept working, and it worked a whole lot better than V-Trak.

That seemed, at the time, like a good enough reason to pursue the subject. And the more I used F-Trak in my whole court game, the more I saw the difference it could make.

But there is an old saying among tennis teachers that goes: Just because it works for you doesn't mean it will work for everybody.

The funny thing is, *everybody* who plays tennis must use their eyes to input visual information to their brain about the movement of the ball. And everybody who uses their eyes to input information to their brain is capable of inputting that information in more than one way. Both V-Trak and F-Trak are input patterns that work for everybody. The question is, which one is the most efficient pattern for tracking a moving object through a given dimension of space and time?

Give F-Trak an honest try, and you will see for yourself.

11

Flash-Outs

As strange as this may sound, the game of tennis can be played without changing your depth of focus. Tell that to a tried-and-true ball-watcher, and you get some funny looks, believe me. But the fact of the matter is, when you fix your focus on your contact zone you can still "see" everything that is happening on the other side of your contact zone. It's just that everything on the other side of your contact zone is out of focus.

This visual reversal takes a little getting used to, but when you think about it, which game sounds more efficient to you: a game where you are continually switching your focus back and forth, trying to keep up with the ball, or a game where you continually keep your focus fixed, and let the ball move in and out of focus?

When I first started experimenting with F-Trak, I found it difficult to keep my focus fixed on my contact zone throughout an entire point. I would start off visualizing a

Shield across my contact zone, but suddenly, I would catch myself focusing on the ball again, or focusing on my opponent, or focusing on where I was going to place my shot.

I started calling these sudden changes in my focus "flash-outs," and flash-outs turned out to be a subtle phenomenon of F-Trak that I found fascinating not only as a teacher, but as a learner as well.

I found that as I practiced controlling my focus I could learn a great deal about my own game by studying exactly what I was flasing out on. Obviously it was something that was drawing my focus, and my attention, away from my Invisible Shield. Something that caused a lapse in my concentration by letting my focus get away. A "flash-out" is a momentary slip in your fixed focus. And the better you get at fixing your focus, the better you get at spotting your flash-outs. Not only what you flashed-out on, but when, during the course of the contact sequence, you flashed-out.

Flash-outs can happen at any time during the contact sequence, and for any number of reasons. The most common flash-outs are:

1. Flashing-out on your opponent.
2. Flashing-out on the ball.
3. Flashing-out on placement.

Flashing-Out on Your Opponent

Flashing-out on your opponent to "see" him hit his shot seems to be the logical thing to do. But, in point of fact, you do not need to focus on your opponent to "see" the shot being made. You can still see everything happening with your focus fixed on your contact zone. It's just out of focus. But when you really think about it, on which Contact Event do you want to be focused — your opponent's or your own? If you think you can keep up with both — try it.

You will soon find out that in many contact sequences the ball, indeed, travels faster than the eye. And when you input inefficient visual information guess what you get for output?

> Garbage-In/Garbage-Out
> Thud! Negative Contact.

Flashing-Out on the Ball

This flash-out occurs with players who are just beginning with F-Trak and have not yet learned to control their focus throughout the course of several consecutive contact sequences. At first it is common to flash-out on the ball just *after* the Contact Event, to "see" where your shot is going. But, again, it is *not* necessary to focus on the ball to see where it is going after you hit it. You will still see where it is going, but as it goes toward its destination it is also going out of focus. You hit it, it goes out of focus. Your opponent hits it, it comes into focus. Back and forth—in and out of focus. It's really quite easy once you get the hang of it. But it does require you to let go of any attachment you have to the ball. Focusing on the ball attaches you do it. The ball becomes the center of your attention, the center of your focus. The better you focus on the ball, the better attached you become to it and to its movement back and forth across the net.

Unfortunately, the movement of the ball back and forth across the net is often too fast for the refocusing capabilities of the human eye. End result:

> Garbage-In/Garbage-Out
> Thud! Negative Contact.

With F-Trak you don't have to worry about staying attached to the ball. In fact, the whole idea is not to be attached to anything but your contact zone. Let your contact zone be the center of your attention – the center of your focus. When you are attached to your contact zone, you are, in one sense of the word, attached to "something," while in another sense, you are attached to "nothing." Focused on something, focused on nothing. In many cultures, the highest form of meditation is one where the mind is freed of all attachments that inhibit the natural flow of the human continuum. "Non-attachment," attached to nothing – what exactly does that mean? How can you be attached to nothing?

Try fixing your focus on your contact zone and you will get an immediate idea of what it feels like to be attached to nothing. You might also find this feeling a little disconcerting at first, but with practice you will see that it is possible to remain unattached to the ball, or your opponent, by simply remaining attached to your contact zone.

Flashing-Out on Placement

How many times have you looked directly at the area of the court where you want your shot to land, only to find that you "saw" the open court very well, but you failed to see contact? End result: Thud! Negative contact.

Looking where you want the ball to go is a flash-out on placement, and it is a common flash-out with players of every level. It is also a visual error that can prove very costly. It is not necessary to focus on the open areas of the court to "see" that they are open. With your focus fixed on your contact zone, you still see the open areas of the court, you are still aware of them, but, as you might expect, they are out of focus. In fact, everything on the other side of your Invisible Shield is out of focus, and with F-Trak, the idea is to keep it that way. It is not necessary to continually refocus your eyes to be aware of what is going on in front of you.

Flash-outs, then, are any unnecessary changes in the focus of your eyes, and the better you get at fixing your focus, the more you will realize that it is possible to see "everything" while being focused on "nothing."

12

Using Your Contact Zone

Motor-Zone Feedback

ONE OF THE MOST INTERESTING DISTINCTIONS BETWEEN DE-sign A and Design B is the distinction between hitting the ball and hitting the Touchpoint on your Invisible Shield. When I teach people how to play tennis in the zone, we play a game called "Motor-Zone Feedback," and it deals directly with the subject of contact.

To play Motor-Zone Feedback, all you need to do is make a slight alteration in your object of contact. In other words, instead of trying to hit the *ball* as many times in a row as possible, see what happens if you hit the Touch-point on your Invisible Shield as many times in a row as possible.

That's all there is to it. Don't worry about *how* you hit the Touchpoint on your Invisible Shield, just hit it, and hit it as many times in a row as you possibly can. Forecourt, mid-court, backcourt, wherever you are on the court, your objective is to hit the Touchpoint on your Invisible Shield. And to give yourself some feedback on how you are doing with Motor-Zone, simply say "Yes" when you hit the Touchpoint, and "No" when you don't.

This game, like all the others, requires you to fix your focus on the contact zone. You can't hit the Touchpoint on your Invisible Shield unless you first create an Invisible Shield across your contact zone. Which means, to play Motor-Zone Feedback, you must first engage your whole brain. It's a challenging mental game, but well worth the effort. You see, when you can distinguish the difference between hitting the ball and hitting the Touchpoint on your Invisible Shield, you will begin to see the difference between making contact in your normal state of consciousness and making contact in a symmetrical state. The difference is dramatic, but you have to experience it yourself. Nobody else can do it for you.

Motor-Zone Feedback is a game full of surprises. The biggest surprise being that you actually *can* distinguish the difference between contacting the ball and contacting the Touchpoint on your Invisible Shield. In fact, you can completely switch to playing a game in which the competition is no longer between you and the ball, but between you

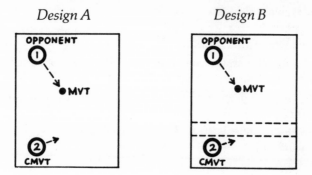

Design A   *Design B*

and your contact zone. Competition takes on a whole new meaning when you stop competing in the past and start competing in the future. And we *are* talking competition here. Both Design A and Design B are designs for counter-movement in a competitive situation. Countermovement, that's you, that's me, that's the person on the other side of the net.

To complete this, or any other contact sequence in tennis, you must make *physical* countermovements that come together at a common point in space and time with the *physical* movement of the ball. That's a physical reality. Contact is a physical happening, and you can make contact happen by hitting the ball, or you can make contact happen by hitting the Touchpoint on your Invisible Shield. Either way the same physical event happens, and that event is what makes the tennis world go 'round. Contact. We all have to make contact. That's a very creative undertaking, requiring a coordinated effort between your eyes, your brain, and your body. Three separate systems working together as one whole system. A whole system capable of tuning itself to different operating modes. "Watch the ball/hit the ball" tunes your system to an asymmetrical mode, but an asymmetrical mode feels normal.

"Look for the Touchpoint/hit the Touchpoint" tunes your system to a symmetrical mode, and a symmetrical mode feels different. Strange at first, a bit spacey. I've had many people tell me they actually felt like they were in a daydream while they were playing. I've had others tell me they can actually "see" their Shield out in front of them. Others see Shields with a tint of color. Some have even told me their Shields have auras around them. While others have told me the whole thing is ridiculous. Playing tennis in the zone is ridiculous, and I must be crazy to tell people they don't have to watch the ball/hit the ball.

But mostly I teach people who are more than willing to

try something different if they think it will help their game, and switching on your whole brain will definitely help your game. When I first started using the Shield as a teaching tool, I was constantly amazed by how fast a player's countermovements developed when I stayed out of the learning process and just let them experiment with contacting the Touchpoint on their Invisible Shield. But when you think about it, experimenting with contacting the Touchpoint on your Invisible Shield is an experiment in creating countermovements that are perfectly timed — whatever they look like on the surface.

You should see how fast a player's individual techniques progress when he starts combining those techniques with Positiming. Or, you can see for yourself what happens to your own techniques when you put them together with Positiming. All you have to do is take your "technique" and use it to hit the Touchpoint on your Invisible Shield. It's as simple as playing tennis in a daydream.

The Movable Shield

One of the first questions I always get asked deals with the concept of a "stationary" or "fixed" contact zone. The question usually goes something like this: "What happens when you are standing in the backcourt and your opponent hits a drop shot into the forecourt? What happens to your stationary contact zone then?"

The answer is simple: You take your Invisible Shield with you as you run forward from the backcourt to the forecourt. Think of it as running toward the drop shot with your Invisible Shield preceding you, leading the way, like a big transparent wall closing in on the ball.

And when your Invisible Shield intercepts the ball, guess what? *That's* the Touchpoint on your Invisible Shield, and *that* is the exact point the ball first enters the space and time of your contact zone: the Touchpoint. Whamee! Look for the Touchpoint/hit the Touchpoint.

As you can imagine, Invisible Shields are highly mobile; they don't weigh very much, and you can take them with you wherever you go on the court. That's the idea. Your Shield is "stationary" in that it always remains arm's-lenth in front of you, perpetually defining the front side of your contact zone. Yet your Shield is also "movable" in that your contact zone always moves with you wherever you go on the court.

Question: What is "stationary" and "movable" at the same time?

Answer: Your future. A constant and a variable, simultaneously. Time moves. Time stands still. Paradox.

The Shield and Lobs

Another point that is generally brought up concerns lobbing the ball *over* your Invisible Shield. What do you do then?

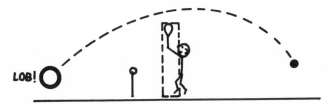

Obviously, your Invisible Shield goes up only so high — as high as you can reach your racket. Or, as high as you can jump up and reach your racket. That would be the maximum height you could conceivably hit the Touchpoint on your Invisible Shield. If your opponent hits the ball any higher than that, it will go over your contact zone, especially if you just stand there and let it go over your contact zone.

Enter the overhead smash — one of the most difficult strokes to master in the game of tennis. But the overhead smash, like any other stroke in tennis, is nothing more than a countermovement made up of technique and timing.

I used to teach people the overhead smash by going into detail about shoulder pivots, racket preparation, the complex footwork patterns, shuffle steps, cross-over steps, scissor kicks. I was especially fond of pointing at the ball with your index finger as you shuffled back for the smash. Of course, pointing at the ball and hitting the ball are two entirely different things. I found that my students had very little trouble pointing at the ball, and, with practice, they had very little trouble with the shuffle steps. The cross-over steps were a little more difficult to learn as a technique, and the scissor kick more difficult still. It was like a progression from beginning overhead technique to intermediate overhead technique to advanced overhead technique. And, all the while I taught my students these various techniques, I wondered why they had so much trouble hitting overheads. What was the problem? Their technique looked pretty good, all the way down to their index fingers. So why do people with supposedly good technique end up producing negative contact on their overhead smash?

Could it be that the timing portion of their overhead countermovement is not equal to the technique portion? Remember, an overhead contact sequence is still a contact sequence containing the essential elements of movement, countermovement, and contact.

First, there is the movement of the ball going over your contact zone, then there is your countermovement to back up and intercept the ball, then there is contact. The event of the ball and your racket coming together at a common point in space and time.

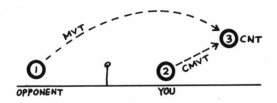

The problem most people have is not a problem of performing the necessary countermovements, but a problem of performing the necessary countermovements in the right amount of time. The overhead smash is just like any other countermovement in that it must relate not only in space to the movement of the ball, but also in time.

When I teach the overhead smash I use a concentrative game that deals with the overhead smash from the point of view of your contact zone. It's a game involving the movable Shield, only instead of taking your Shield with you as you move forward for a drop shot, you simply take your Shield with you as you back up for a lob.

Objective: Back up and don't let the ball get over your Invisible Shield. In other words, instead of backing up and swinging at the ball, the idea is to back your Shield up and swing at the Touchpoint.

In an overall sense, the idea is to let nothing get past your Invisible Shield. Move your Invisible Shield forward to intercept drop shots; move your Invisible Shield backward to intercept lobs. As you move your Shield forward or back, keep looking for the Touchpoint, and when you see it, hit it! That's the exact point the ball first enters the space and time of your contact zone, as good a place as any to create a contact event, especially an overhead Contact Event. In fact, if you back your Shield up and hit the Touchpoint, you have effectively created an overhead countermovement that is absolutely positimed—even if you get your shuffle steps mixed up with your scissor kick.

DESIGN B

Serve Returns and the Half-Shield

The serve return, like the serve itself, is your introduction into the point, and, as such, it is a very important part of your game. But, as we all know, the serve return is easily botched. Why is that? You know your opponent must serve the ball into the correct service court, and you know that if he doesn't, the serve is a fault, and you don't have to make positive contact.

This logic narrows things down considerably. In terms of your contact zone it narrows things down by approximately half. In other words, a "half-shield" is ready made for the serve return.

Diagram A depicts the angle your opponent can hit his serve and still land the ball in the service court.

Diagram B depicts an Invisible Shield spanning the width of approximately half the court. This "half-shield" represents the full width of your contact zone for the serve return sequence. Simply visualize your "half-shield" arm's-length in front of you, and when your opponent serves the ball — look for the Touchpoint/hit the Touchpoint.

Diagram C depicts what it looks like *before* your opponent serves the ball, and if you take a very close look at Diagram C, you will notice that as you are standing in your ready position waiting for the serve, your eyes are *not* focused on the ball. They are focused on your contact zone.

This visual premise goes radically against the traditional concept of "watching the ball" on the serve return. A concept that I grew up with and struggled with, just like every other kid who took up tennis. But "watching the ball" on the serve return is just like watching the ball on any other stroke. It is a variable focus tracking pattern (V-Trak), requiring you to refocus from far vision to near vision as you track the ball along its flight line.

Diagram A   *Diagram B*

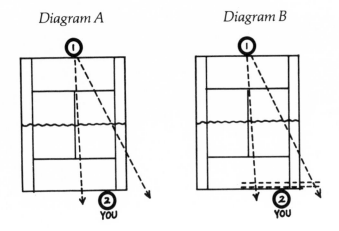

Diagram C

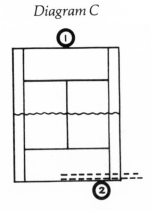

Looking for the Touchpoint on your Invisible Shield is a fixed focus tracking pattern (F-Trak) which does not require you to refocus from far vision to near vision because you are already prefocused for near vision as you track the Touchpoint on your Invisible Shield.

[85]

Both V-Trak and F-Trak are tracking patterns you can use during the serve return sequence, and both patterns require you to focus on something. V-Trak (watch the ball) requires you to focus on the *ball* during the serve return sequence. F-Trak (look for the Touchpoint on your Invisible Shield) requires you to focus on your *contact zone* during the serve return sequence.

Both patterns work, but like any contact sequence, the more efficient the visual input, the more efficient the motor output. That part stays the same, whether you are returning a drop shot or a cannonball serve. And the most direct method of creating a positive output pattern with your body is to create a positive input pattern with your eyes. F-Trak. There it is again. A fixed focus tracking pattern versus a variable focus tracking pattern. Input relative to output. Which pattern inputs the necessary information with the fewest number of variables?

Returning a cannonball serve, or a spin serve, or an American twist serve, or a dink second serve, any serve, left-handed or righthanded, involves your eyes, your brain, and your body, solving the problem of positive contact.

Watch the ball/hit the ball is one pattern for solving the problem.

Look for the Touchpoint/hit the Touchpoint is another.

One is based on a variable. One is based on a constant.

One is Design A. One is Design B.

The question is, which one is more efficient?

Learning to control your focus during the serve return sequence does not mean you will return every serve your opponent hits. It will, however, give you a way to predefine the depth of your contact event for every serve your opponent hits. In other words, no matter what type of serve your opponent hits, be it slice, flat, or twist, the movement of the ball will at some point along its flight line come together with your half-shield.

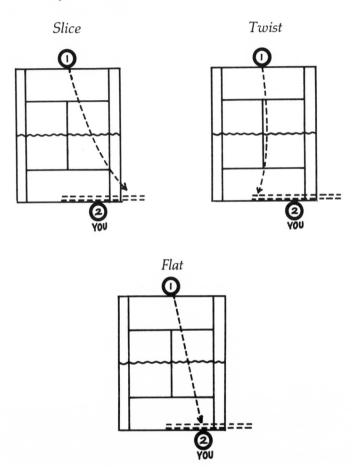

When I teach people to return serve, the first thing we work on is establishing control of the contact zone, no matter what type of serve the opponent hits. The theory being, contact is contact. It will be either positive or negative, and if you create a Contact Event at the exact moment the ball enters your contact zone, your odds for Positive Contact are increased. And it doesn't matter how the ball is spinning or how fast it is going. Your objective in Design B is to look for the Touchpoint/hit the Touchpoint. Once a player learns to control his focus on the serve return, it doesn't take long before he starts controlling his contact zone on the serve return. And, once again, the better you control your contact zone, the more often you make Positive Contact.

Design B and Kids

Imagine you are a kid, never played tennis before, and suddenly you are standing on a great big tennis court, with a funny feeling tennis racket in your hands, and a big person telling you how to grip the racket, then how to swing it back into what's called a "forehand backswing," and then how to pivot your feet and take what are called "crossover steps," and then how to swing your racket at the ball from low to high and finish in what's called a "forehand follow-through."

"There, kid. Got it? It's called a forehand ground stroke. First we learn the forehand ground stroke, then we learn the backhand ground stroke, then the forehand and backhand volley, the serve, the lob, and finally the overhead."

Sound familiar? We teach our kids to play the game the same way we learned to play the game ourselves. Tennis teaching throughout the years has shown a tremendously accelerated evolution, but the basic approach is still the same—linear. Whether teaching adults or kids, the approach is to break the technique down into a linear series of steps that can be followed to the letter, thus producing a letter-perfect technique.

So what you end up seeing is a bunch of little kids lined

up behind their teacher, and suddenly everybody pivots, runs over to the right a few steps, stops, swings to a perfect follow-through, then shuffles back to their original position. It looks great, and, indeed, the kids are learning the basic linear steps involved in their ground strokes. Those steps are being ingrained in their minds, the idea being: If you do the countermovement enough times, you can finally do it without thinking about it. The basic stroking machine: flawless technique.

Question: How do you teach a stroking machine flawless timing? Especially when the stroking machine is four feet tall, six years old, and a little bit scared.

Imagine you are a kid again, and imagine you have the imagination of a kid again. You have never played tennis before, and suddenly you are standing in a great big magic kingdom filled with magic things like invisible castles and magic swords, and tall dragons who spit fireballs at your invisible castle wall. Your objective: Take the flat side of your magic sword and make sure no fireballs burn a hole in your castle wall.

When you give all those magic pieces an objective you come up with a fairy tale a kid can relate to a lot easier than backswings, crossover steps, and follow throughs.

The funny thing is, this fairy tale contains the fundamentals of movement, countermovement, and contact, just like the real game of tennis, and when you take your magic sword and make sure no fireballs burn a hole in your invisible castle wall, you end up with a fairy tale game that looks amazingly similar to the game of tennis.

Kids catch on to the visualization part immediately. After all, who daydreams better than kids? Invisible castle walls are easy to visualize for a six-year-old, and it doesn't take long before they become very adept at looking for the "Burnpoint" on their invisible castle wall. End result — a six-year-old kid using a fixed focus tracking pattern instead of a variable focus tracking pattern.

Simply switching the object of focus from the fireball to the contact zone, not only is a more efficient visual input pattern starting to develop (F-Trak), but there is also a more efficient motor output pattern starting to develop (Motor-Zone).

Most importantly, however, is what starts to develop cognitively when a six-year-old learns how to use his whole brain to solve the problem of Positive Contact. Kids are naturals at it. It's easy for them to play "daydream tennis," and the results are the same as grown-up results. Every time a six-year-old hits the burnpoint with the flat side of his magic sword, he creates a Contact Event at the exact point the tennis ball first enters the space and time of his six-year-old contact zone. His swordsmanship may not be "biomechanically sound" just yet, but, for a six-year-old, he's got great timing! And when it comes to countermovement, it doesn't matter if you are six or sixty, your countermovements are still an equal combination of technique and timing.

$$\frac{\text{Technique}}{\text{Timing}} = \text{Countermovement}$$

A six-year-old hitting the burnpoint with his magic sword is a six-year-old making countermovements that form a positive relationship in space and time with the movement of the "fireball." That's a nice place to start when it comes to teaching tennis to kids—and grown-ups.

13

Symmetry

DESIGN B HAS BEEN FUN TO DEVELOP AS A TEACHING METHOD because it involves so many different levels. On one level it involves science: the physics of movement — countermovement — contact, and the space/time relationships of the contact sequence. On another level it involves the human visual/cognitive/motor system being tuned to a different operating mode, a mode of symmetrical cooperation between the eyes, the brain, and the body. On yet another level Design B involves consciousness, on-court visualization, the coexistence of the real and the imaginary, concentration, focus, and the mind.

But however many levels Design B involves, people seem to get out of it what they want. For some, that means nothing more than a working concept of good timing, which isn't a bad way to start fixing what's wrong with your game. For others, however, Design B has been a means for investigating their own potential both on the court and off. A means for investigating the mysteries of their own minds.

Learning to control your focus doesn't sound like much in today's world of sound biomechanical technique and computerized stick printouts. But Design B doesn't involve fancy technology. Invisible Shields are about as far from fancy technology as you can get.

Instead, Design B involves you, doing something with your eyes that brings about a very special happening.

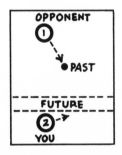

When you visualize an imaginary Shield across your contact zone you create a situation on the tennis court in which two separate realities exist simultaneously: the reality of the ball and the reality of your contact zone. Separate realities in every sense of the word. Opposing realities. One is visible, one invisible. One real, one imaginary. One is Past Space, one is Future Space. The ball and the contact zone: the past and the future, existing together in the space and time of every contact sequence.

Think about it. When you look for the Touchpoint on your Invisible Shield you are literally "seeing" the past and the future simultaneously. And by bringing together these two opposing realities you create a third reality — the most subtle reality of all. It runs along the thinnest of lines, balanced on the leading edge of time; it is fleeting, elusive, the third reality.

Question: Where are you when you are "in the past" and "in the future" simultaneously?

The answer to that question is what Design B is all about. You see, Design B is about a lot of things, but, in the end, it's about being "in the present." That's the reality you actively create when you look for the Touchpoint on your Invisible Shield. A reality which combines the past and the future simultaneously.

The "simultaneously" part is what's important. When seen separately, the past and the future are opposing realities, the asymmetrical halves of a symmetrical whole.

When seen simultaneously, however, the past and the future are brought together, creating the present, the asymmetrical halves combining to create a "symmetrical whole."

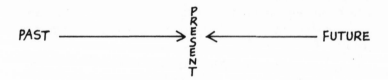

Have you ever thought about what it really means to be "in the present"? What is the present? What is it made up of? It certainly goes by in a hurry! How do you link up with it? How do you become "one" with the present? Sounds like a nice place to be, but is it all a bunch of philosophical mumbo-jumbo? Or is it real? Can you really exist "in the present"? Is it possible to be in time with time itself?

Do you care?

There are lots of people who don't, but there is also a growing number who do. People who are into their own consciousness, their own being. People in search of the harmony of mind and body. The concept of being "in the present" is a mind-boggler. A philosophical quandary of baffling paradox. Yet, in all its wondrous complexity, being in the present is as simple as child's play.

So is Design B.

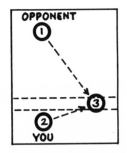

Look for the Touchpoint on your Invisible Shield.
Hit the Touchpoint on your Invisible Shield.
Child's play.

14

Serving in the Zone

The Serving Sequence

DESIGN B WOULD NOT BE COMPLETE WITHOUT A SECTION ON
the serving sequence, a.k.a. "serving in the zone." And serving in the zone is easy once you have an idea of what your "serving zone" looks like.

But first of all, what constitutes a serving sequence?

MOVEMENT →COUNTERMOVEMENT →CONTACT

First comes the movement of the ball – the toss – then comes countermovement – the swing – then comes contact – the event of the ball and your racket coming together at a common point in space and time.

Look familiar? It should. The serving sequence, in base form, is a contact sequence containing a relationship in space and time between movement and countermovement.

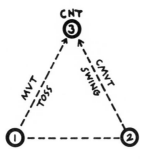

This relationship is competitive. It pits the movement of the ball — your toss — against your countermovements to intercept the ball — your swing. Movement versus countermovement, the toss versus the swing. Objective: contact.

Oops! That's not the real objective, is it? Anybody can make contact on their serve. The real objective is Positive Contact. Your serve has to land within the given dimensions of the service court, and that takes Positive Contact.

When I work with people on their serve, Positive Contact becomes the main objective, and in the serving sequence Positive Contact is the end result of a positive relationship between movement and countermovement.

$$\frac{MVT(+)}{CMVT(+)} = CNT(+)$$

This simple formula translates to: A good toss and a good swing equals good contact. Not exactly earth-shattering as formulas go, but it does allow for a conceptual understanding of what it takes to produce a Positive Contact event on your serve, as well as what it takes to produce a Negative Contact event on your serve.

Here are four formulas for producing a Contact Event in the serving sequence:

A. $\dfrac{\text{MVT}\,(+)}{\text{CMVT}\,(+)} = \text{CNT}\,(++)$

$\dfrac{\text{Positive Toss}}{\text{Positive Swing}} = \text{Positive Contact}$

B. $\dfrac{\text{MVT}\,(-)}{\text{CMVT}\,(+)} = \text{CNT}\,(-+)$

$\dfrac{\text{Negative Toss}}{\text{Positive Swing}} = \text{Variable Contact}$

C. $\dfrac{\text{MVT}\,(+)}{\text{CMVT}\,(-)} = \text{CNT}\,(+-)$

$\dfrac{\text{Positive Toss}}{\text{Negative Swing}} = \text{Variable Contact}$

D. $\dfrac{\text{MVT}\,(-)}{\text{CMVT}\,(-)} = \text{CNT}\,(--)$

$$\frac{\text{Negative Toss}}{\text{Negative Swing}} = \text{Negative Contact}$$

If this was a multiple choice question on what constitutes a positive serving sequence, obviously your answer would be Formula A.

But if this was a multiple choice question on the constitution of your *own* serving sequence, then which formula would you choose?

The serving sequence is similar to any contact sequence in that it contains movement, countermovement, and contact, but in a forehand contact sequence, or a backhand contact sequence, your *opponent* is responsible for producing the positive movement of the ball in your direction.

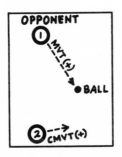

All you have to do is supply the positive countermovement portion of the formula—a good swing.

In a serving sequence, however, you, as the server, are in charge of producing both positive movement (a good toss) *and* positive countermovement (a good swing).

In serving, the whole contact sequence is literally in your hands. In one hand you have the object of movement, and

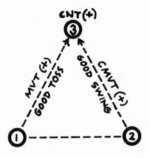

in the other hand you have the object of countermovement. It should be simple enough to bring those two objects together in a Positive Contact Event, yet serving is perhaps the most difficult stroke to master. Why is that? As a tennis teacher I have faced that question for many years, and for most of that time I thought the answer was in teaching people a sound serving technique. Unfortunately, defining a sound serving technique involves quite a long linear progression of individual countermovements that all add up to the "biomechanically sound" serving motion. This, again, is the traditional approach to teaching the serve. The linear approach. First you learn how to toss, then you learn how to swing, then you learn how to toss and swing all at the same time. And *that's* when things get all fouled up. The toss and the swing are easy to understand as individual linear progressions, but bringing them together in space and time is what serving is all about. Your toss and your swing must form a positive relationship in space and time in order to create a Positive Contact Event.

$$\frac{\text{MVT}\,(+)}{\text{CNVT}\,(+)} = \text{CNT}\,(+)$$

So how do you go about creating a positive relationship between your toss and your swing?

When I first started investigating the idea of defining the contact zone with my focus, it made sense that the same concept could be used for defining the spatial dimensions of the serving zone.

In other words, it is possible to prefocus on your serving zone in the same manner you prefocus on your contact zone. Just as you can give your contact zone the physical "shape" of a large Plexiglas window, you can also give your serving zone a physical shape that will help you understand the concept of serving in the zone.

Here's what I mean: Imagine yourself standing arm's-length away from a wall—or the backdrop at your club.

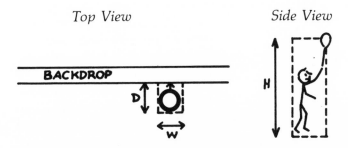

Top View   *Side View*

In the top view, the imaginary dotted lines represent the width and depth of your serving zone. The width is slightly wider than your own shoulders. The depth is arm's-length in front of you.

The height of your serving zone can be seen with a side view: Your serving zone extends to the height you can reach your racket.

The overall picture of your serving zone is that of a large, invisible box, rectangular in shape, and since everyone is a different size, everyone's serving zone is also a different size. So one of the first things I do with someone

who is having problems with his serve is have him visualize the size and shape of his own serving zone.

When I first applied Design B to serving, I used the same 3-2-1 measuring system I had used to define the different depths of the contact zone. A 3-depth is full arm's-length in front of you, a 2-depth is elbow's-length in front of you, and a 1-depth is even with your body.

The same 3-2-1 measuring system can be used to define the height of your serving zone. A 3-height being the highest point you can reach your racket on the front side of your serving zone, a 2-height being just below that, and a 1-height slightly lower.

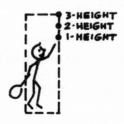

Just as my contact zone had a front side, a middle, and a back side, it was logical that my serving zone would also have a front side, middle, and back side. Likewise, I could use an Invisible Shield to represent the front side of my serving zone in the same way I used it to represent the front side of my contact zone.

The point of maximum extension in your own serving zone can be measured as a 3-height/3-depth: the 3-point. The highest point you can reach your racket on the front side of your serving zone.

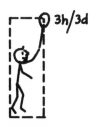

These height, width, and depth measurements are important because they can help you measure exactly where the Contact Event occurs in your serving zone. When I watch someone serving, I don't analyze his serving motion to see what is wrong with his technique. Rather I observe the exact location of the Contact Event in his serving zone. I can still "see" his technique, but by measuring the location of contact, I get a very objective view of his technique as it relates to his serving zone.

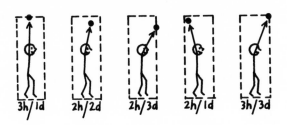

Here is a typical view of five consecutive Contact Events for a player who is having trouble with his serve.

If you happen to be having trouble with your own serve, you might find there are some very logical reasons why your serve is going out, as well as some very logical ways to get your serve to go in. But instead of analyzing your serving motion (which is probably well within the parameters of traditionally accepted technique), try observing the "location" of your contact. See where contact occurs within the dimensions of your predefined serving zone. Don't worry about *how* you hit your serve, just give your contact an objective measurement.

At first you might find it difficult to pinpoint the exact location of contact, but as you practice, you will begin to expand your awareness of the dimensions of your serving zone, along with getting a very honest look at how well your toss and your swing relate to your serving zone.

If you are like most people, you will probably find that your contact occurs at a variety of locations in your serving zone. Don't feel bad. It happens to everybody, and there are some very logical ways to correct a variable contact location. The first is to correct the variable location of your toss. In other words, in order to create a Contact Event at the optimum location in your serving zone, it is first necessary to deliver the ball to that optimum location.

The 1 Flight-Line Toss

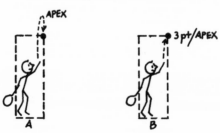

Here are two diagrams of a toss. In both diagrams the movement of the ball has been delivered to the Optimum Contact Point — the 3-point. But, as you can see, the lines of delivery are considerably different. Diagram A is an example of a "2 flight-line toss," while Diagram B is an example of a "1 flight-line toss."

Most players have been taught the 2 flight-line toss, but, when you look at what it takes to successfully complete a 2 flight-line toss, you find that before your toss will come down correctly every time, it must first go up correctly every time. Which involves tossing the ball consistently to the same apex — Point X in Diagram A.

Such tossing consistency is not inconceivable, it's just practically impossible! Unless, of course, you are an exceptionally good tosser.

How often do you think you could hit this imaginary apex with your toss?

Next question, how often do you think you could hit *this* imaginary apex with your toss?

I don't know about you, but for me the closer the target, the easier it is to hit it with my toss. So instead of tossing for a target that is located *outside* the dimensions of my serving zone, I have found it much easier to control my toss when my target is located *within* the dimensions of my serving zone. Think of it as tossing "in the zone."

In the end, the name of the game in tossing is accuracy. If you can consistently deliver the ball to the optimum contact point (3-height/3-depth), your chances for Positive Contact are considerably increased. And nowhere in the rules does it say you are required to use a 2 flight-line toss to deliver the ball to the Optimum Contact Point. It just says *you* have to toss it, and *you* have to hit it. It also says you have to hit it in, which means you have to create Positive Contact. That's what serving is all about — Positive Contact. But Positive Contact, remember, is the end result of a positive relationship between movement and counter-movement.

$$\frac{MVT\,(+)}{CMVT\,(+)} = CNT\,(+)$$

By tossing the ball on one line to the 3-point, you will be completing the positive movement portion of the formula as efficiently as possible. The 1-flight line toss. It is the first step to serving "in the zone."

1 Flight-Line Equals 1 Flight-Time

The idea of a 1 flight-line toss is to keep the movement of the ball within the predefined spatial dimensions of your serving zone. That way, not only is it easier to control the flight-*line* of your toss, it is also easier to control the flight-*time* of your toss. It takes a certain amount of time for the ball to move from the tossing point to the Optimum Contact Point.

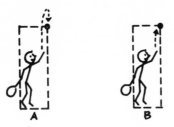

Give these diagrams some motion and you can see that the 2 flight-line toss is also a 2 flight-time toss. It takes X amount of time for the ball to go up, and X amount of time for the ball to come down, giving you a total flight-time that is always a combination of X-up and X-down.

$$TFT = (X\uparrow) + (X\downarrow)$$

The 1 flight-line toss, by contrast, is also a 1 flight-time toss. Which means the total flight time of your toss is equal to the upward flight-time of your toss (X-up).

$$TFT = (X\uparrow)$$

When seen together, the difference in total flight-time becomes apparent. The 2 flight-line toss obviously takes longer to arrive at the optimum contact point than the 1 flight-line toss, which doesn't make the 2 flight-line toss wrong, it just makes the 2 flight-line toss more difficult to reproduce time after time after time. Good tossing means consistency — tossing the ball through the same amount of space in the same amount of time, every time. You do a lot of tossing over the course of a complete match, and the more consistently you deliver the movement of the ball to the Optimum Contact Point, the more consistently you will be able to delivery the countermovements of your racket to the Optimum Contact Point. End result: more consistent contact at the Optimum Contact Point.

This does not mean your serve will go in every time, but consistently creating a contact event at the Optimum Contact Point will certainly raise your odds.

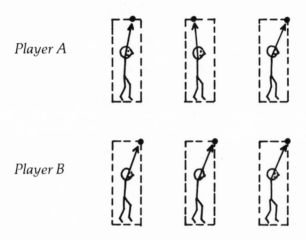

Player A

Player B

Which player do you think has the best odds for creating Positive Contact in the serving sequence?

Player A, whose 2 flight-line toss is often inaccurate, causing the Contact Event to occur at variable locations within his serving zone?

Or, Player B, whose 1 flight-line toss consistently goes to the same location, allowing contact to occur at the optimum location within his serving zone?

My money is on Player B, even if his technique is ridiculous. You see, Player B might have a completely unorthodox serving motion, but if that unorthodox serving motion starts creating contact at the 3-point, then Player B has an unorthodox serving motion that is absolutely positimed.

In two decades of teaching and playing tennis you see a lot of unorthodox serving techniques, and having spent the better part of my formative years on the public courts, I assure you there are thousands of highly competent tennis players with ridiculous serving techniques. Orthodoxy is not what makes something "right." It took me a long time to understand exactly what that means, both as a player and as a teacher. I've had a great deal more success teaching people how to serve since I stopped trying to explain the serve in terms of technique, and started explaining the serve in terms of the serving zone.

People get the hang of tossing the ball to the 3-point in a hurry. It is really very easy compared with launching the ball somewhere up above you and hoping it comes down in the general vicinity of your Optimum Contact Point.

The funny thing is, once a player starts delivering his toss to the same target every time, he finds that his toss takes the same amount of time to get to the target every time. It gets a little repetitious after awhile — toss to the 3-point . . . toss to the 3-point . . . toss to the 3-point . . . the same thing, every time. You should see how fast a player gets control of the timing portion of his countermovements when he has a constant amount of time to work with, time, after time, after time. I don't have to tell him much about his technique, once he learns how to positime it.

F-Trak and the Serve

No matter what technique you use to serve the ball, there is something even more fundamental going on than your technique. Something that is far more important to Positive Contact than how you swing your racket. Think about it. Beneath the surface of your serving technique lies the fundamental visual/cognitive/motor pattern you use to operate your overall system. Like any other contact sequence in tennis, the serving sequence gives you the choice of using a variable focus tracking pattern to input information to your brain about the movement of the ball (V-Trak). Or, you can use a fixed focus tracking pattern to input information to your brain about the ball and the contact zone simultaneously (F-Trak). All you do is fix your focus on the 3-point (3-height/3-depth) *before* you toss the ball. That's important to remember. Here's what it looks like:

Looks pretty strange, doesn't it? Standing there staring at open space. Your opponent will probably wonder what you are looking at. He might also wonder why you aren't looking at the ball. Of course, with F-Trak the visual objective is not to "watch the ball." Rather, the idea is to use your eyes to predefine the future point of contact. Future-focus again. By fixing your focus on the 3-point before you toss the ball, you are simultaneously focusing on the future point of your toss (movement), the future point of your swing (countermovement), and the future point of the contact event (contact). That makes three future-points in one future-point. The 3-point. It is by far the most important point in the whole serving sequence. The 3-point, however, is invisible. But, as you know by now, it is quite within the range of human capability to focus on the invisible. It all boils down to controlling the focus of your eyes in the serving sequence.

Tossing the ball to the 3-point is easy when you are looking straight at the 3-point before you toss the ball. It's like looking at a target before you throw something at it. The problem most people face is that they toss the ball, then use their eyes to track the flight line of the ball. The assumption being, that the better they watch the ball the better they will hit it. Absolutely correcto. The better the visual input, the better the motor output. The real problem, however, is that watching the ball along its flight line does not make the flight line of your toss correct. A crummy toss is a crummy toss no matter how well you watch it. And watching the ball closer will not make your toss any better.

Here is an imaginary situation that will explain the difference between V-Trak and F-Trak in the serving sequence. Imagine standing arm's-length away from a Plexiglas window that has a great big "X" painted at the location of your 3-point.

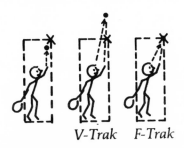

V-Trak   F-Trak

Now imagine you are in a simple contest in which you must toss the ball to the location marked with the X.

Question: If the object of your toss is to hit the X with the ball, what would you look at — the ball, or the target?

You don't need to know the answer to that question. You can try it and see for yourself. Stand arm's-length away from a backdrop, a fence, or a wall, and reach your racket to the highest point you can on the surface of the wall. That's your 3-point — the highest point you can reach your racket on the front side of your serving zone.

Now, see how close you can toss the ball to your target *without looking at the target*. Take as many practice tosses as you need, but no fair looking at the target! You have to "watch the ball," remember?

Try it a hundred times and see how often you can hit the target while you watch the ball. You might even try some 2 flight line tosses. That way, you can watch the ball go up, and you can watch the ball come down. You will also see how often the downward flight line of the ball hits your target. Or, how seldom.

When I show beginners how to toss the ball for their serve, I use this same backdrop analogy, only I don't show them any "biomechanically sound" technique for tossing the ball. Tossing a ball is not biomechanically difficult. And what makes it a good toss is not whether it looks good, but whether it goes to the right spot. So all I do is have beginners target their 3-point on the backdrop, and then see how close they can come to it with their toss.

Guess what they do? They immediately look straight at the target on the backdrop, and start tossing the ball at it. Intuitively, they do *not* watch the ball. They watch the target instead, and in a very short time, without any assistance from me, they are consistently tossing the ball very close to their target.

Try it yourself. Give it a hundred chances and you will see that focusing on your target *before* you toss the ball makes the target considerably easier to hit with the ball.

Given one hundred tries, you will quite probably get bored, but you will also develop a toss that delivers the ball through the same amount of space in the same amount of time, every time. That's a good toss. Too bad you can't paint a great big "X" on your serving zone to predefine your 3-point. That way you would have a visible target on which to focus your eyes before you toss the ball. Think how much easier it would be to hit the target if you actually had a target to focus on. Of course, you could always *pretend* you have a great big "X" painted on your serving zone. That would certainly give you something to focus on, even if it is imaginary.

But real or imaginary, what's the difference in this case? The idea is to target the 3-point with your eyes, and for that you don't need real paint. The mind's eye is extraordinarily artistic.

Motor-Zone and the Serve

This section deals with the countermovement portion of the serving sequence, the swing portion of the formula for positive contact.

$$\frac{MVT\ (+)}{CMVT\ (+)} = CNT\ (+)$$

$$\frac{Positive\ Toss}{Positive\ Swing} = Positive\ Contact$$

I used to teach people how to serve by going through all the bends in all the joints, and all the weight transfers, J-tosses, throwing motions, half-serves, full serves, toes pointed this way, shoulders rotated that way, it was amazing how many details I could cram into a serving lesson.

And all the while I stood there wondering why my students couldn't make Positive Contact more often. After all, every technique I showed them was proven biomechanically sound by a team of experts in Florida. So why didn't it work?

Maybe teacher wasn't teaching so well. Maybe teacher was teaching too much. The quality was okay, but the quantity was confusing. The serve is one of those strokes that can be broken down into an incredible number of linear parts, each one contributing in its own way to the linear whole. But is the object of teaching to teach the "parts," or the "whole"?

When I work with a player on his serve, the last thing on my mind is the notion of picking apart the flaws in his swing. Individual flaws in technique do not make inconsistent servers. The problem is more basic than that; it is more deeply imbedded in the structure of the serving sequence. It has to do with the relationship between simultaneous occurrences. The "line of movement" and the "line of countermovement" must form a positive relationship within a given amount of space and time. If they do not, your odds for Negative Contact increase.

Nowadays, instead of trying to show people what is wrong with the "parts" of their swing, I try to show them how their "whole" swing relates to the space and time of their serving zone. Which means the person must first visualize an imaginary serving zone before he can "see" how the line of his toss and the line of his swing relate to his own Optimum Contact Point.

That's an important step the player must take on his own, but the best thing is, the instant someone starts visualizing his serving zone, a change in the learning process immediately starts to occur. A change in which the "whole-brain" is brought into the act of learning. And when that happens, learning is no longer "being taught."

Instead, learning is discovery, awareness, excitement. I don't have to do much once the discovery part takes hold. In fact, that's when I step back and let go as a teacher. Any suggestions I make deal directly with an objective measurement of the serving sequence as it relates to the player's individual serving zone.

To do this I have had to train myself to stop watching the player and start watching his serving zone. In other words, I stand behind the server and visualize his serving zone.

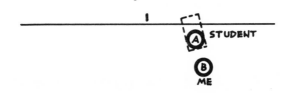

If the student is willing to try something different, he too will be visualizing his serving zone. Which means we are both fixing our focus on exactly the same thing—which is "nothing." Or is it "something"?

How exactly does one classify the serving zone? Is it something that is nothing? Or nothing that is something? Or is it both simultaneously? It is easy to visualize your serving zone as you read about it, but the idea is to visualize your serving zone during the actual serving sequence. To use your serving zone as both a visual and physical aid to Positive Contact on your serve.

By the way, your serving zone is very hard to visualize if you watch the ball on your toss. However, your serving zone is easy to visualize if you fix your focus on it. And when you visualize your serving zone, you get the bonus of "seeing" your Optimum Contact Point. Something that is very difficult to do when you watch the ball. Of course, if the downward flight line of the ball happens to cross the 3-point, then you will "see" the Optimum Contact Point. However, by then it is too late. You see, the Optimum Contact Point is also the Optimum contact Time, and the Optimum Contact Time doesn't hang around for long. Milliseconds again. So, in the end, it really doesn't make very good sense to watch the ball on your serve. Your eyes aren't helping you; they are, in a sense, following the action and reporting home. That's a very passive visual pattern—past-focus from start to finish.

By contrast, fixing your focus on the front side of your serving zone is a visual pattern in which you use your eyes to actively create the Optimum Contact Point as a target for both your toss and your swing. Future-focus from start to finish.

You might be surprised how quickly the line of your toss and the line of your swing start forming a positive relationship once you give them the same future.

Alignment

Like any other contact sequence in tennis, the serving sequence comes to its positive or negative completion at the Contact Event. What occurs in the milliseconds that compose the lifespan of a contact event determines the positive or negative outcome of the entire movement/counter-movement relationship. It all boils down to contact again, and in a symmetrical serving sequence, your focus is on contact, because that's where and when it all comes together. And when it all comes together, it *looks* like something, except it is hard to see exactly what the Contact Event looks like, because it happens so fast. But thanks to slow motion and stop action photography, some very basic characteristics of contact can be seen.

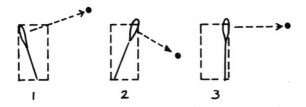

When I say very basic, I mean very basic. If your strings are pointed up at contact, the ball goes up. If your strings are pointed down, the ball goes down. If your strings are pointed straight ahead, the ball goes straight ahead. Each of these serves eventually has to come down, and, according to the rules, the ball must come down within the given dimensions of the service court.

Two of the above Contact Events contain the physical characteristics necessary for Positive Contact in the serving sequence. Number one can produce Positive Contact if you don't hit it too hard. If you hit it too hard, number one can hit the back fence.

Number two will definitely *not* produce Positive Contact, unless, of course, you are very, very tall, or have an exceptionally good vertical leap.

Number three, however, contains the physical characteristics necessary for Positive Contact without the power variable of number one or the vertical leap variable of number two. In other words, if your strings are pointed straight ahead at contact, gravity takes care of the rest.

Most players don't have as much trouble with the direction of their serve as they do hitting it too long or too short. That's a depth problem, and it is a problem that is directly related to the vertical alignment of your strings at contact.

Try standing approximately arm's-length away from the backdrop and swing your racket up and flat into your

3-point. You will get a resounding "thwack" when your racket is flat at contact.

THWACKO!

This of course does not give you a true feeling of the entire service motion because you can't follow through. It does, however, give you a true feeling of the service motion up to the point of contact. Which is the part that counts! Besides, the natural follow through that results from a swing extending to the highest point you can reach on the front side of your serving zone is a follow through that looks very much like what a follow through should look like.

In terms of the serving sequence itself the follow through comes *after* the Contact Event, which means you can have a biomechanically sound follow through, or a biomechanically ridiculous follow through, it doesn't matter, the ball has already left your strings.

If someone is having trouble controlling the depth of his serve, it is usually because of simple physical reasons like his strings are pointed up at contact, so his serve goes long, or his strings are pointed down at contact so his serve goes into the net. Nothing mysterious there. Likewise, there is nothing mysterious about why the serve goes wide-left or wide-right. If it goes wide-left it is usually because your strings are pointed too far to the left. If you miss to the right, it is usually because your strings are pointed too far to the right. This is known as "horizontal alignment," and it works together with vertical alignment to produce a contact event with positive or negative direction.

When I describe a player's serving zone to him, I make sure he understands that the front side of his serving zone is a *flat* surface like the surface of a backdrop or a window. A flat surface provides a "control" for your swing that is both visual and physical, and this control can be used to keep your contact vertically and horizontally aligned when you serve.

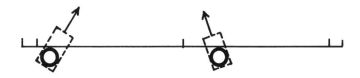

Once you visualize your serving zone, you can set it up wherever you set up to serve on the baseline. By using your imagination you can actually "point" your serving zone in the direction of either service court. So no matter where you stand on the baseline, you can predefine the exact height, width, and depth of your Optimum Contact Point.

The thing is, flat surfaces and tennis go together. Your tennis racket is a flat surface, and your Invisible Shield is a flat surface. Swing one flat surface flat through the other flat surface, and you've got a Contact Event that is horizontally and vertically aligned.

Future-Focus and the Serve

What does all this Future-Focus jazz have to do with serving? I've had more than one student look at me funny when I suggest they focus on an imaginary point located within the dimensions of an imaginary serving zone.

"But there's nothing there to focus on!" they say, pointing at their 3-point.

Therein lies one of the mysteries of future-focus. You see, as long as you believe there is nothing there to focus on, then you are right, there is nothing there to focus on. But once you start visualizing your own serving zone, you begin to realize there really *is* something there! And you *can* focus on it! The 3-point does, in fact, exist. And by focusing on it, you bring it to life, and when you bring your 3-point to life, you bring to life the future point of the whole serving sequence.

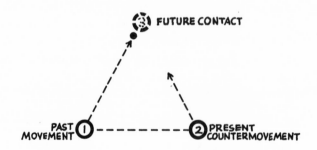

By fixing your focus on the future, you are again creating a situation in which you "see" the past and the future simultaneously. Guess where that puts you in the space and time of every serving sequence?

$$\frac{Past}{Future} = Present$$

Serving in the zone means serving "in the present." And you get into the present by combining the past and the future in a simultaneous flow of time. The past and the future coming together to form the present. *Your* present. You create it yourself. Nobody else can do it for you. The funny thing is, it's as simple as bringing your imagination into the reality of the serving sequence.

Diagram A

Toss the Ball
Watch the Ball
Hit the Ball

Diagram B

Focus on the 3-Point
Toss to the 3-Point
Hit the 3-Point

Diagram A represents the traditional serving sequence in which you toss the ball/watch the ball/hit the ball. Or, if you are a devout V-Traker, you first watch the ball, then you toss the ball/hit the ball.

Diagram B represents serving in the zone; a slightly altered serving sequence in which you first fix your focus on the 3-point, then you toss to the 3-point/hit the 3-point.

Both patterns for the serving sequence produce a contact

event between the ball and your racket. One pattern, however, Pattern B, engages both hemispheres of the brain in a symmetrical processing mode throughout the course of the serving sequence.

Pattern A also engages both hemispheres, but in a dominant/subordinate mode — asymmetrical cognitive processing from start to finish. In other words, Pattern A is the pattern for serving in your normal state of consciousness; a half-brain dominant state.

Pattern B is *not* a pattern for serving in your normal state of consciousness, because in order to complete Pattern B, you must first switch on your whole brain. And to do that, you must alter your state of consciousness. That's where visualizing your imaginary 3-point comes in. By visualizing your 3-point you actively engage the subordinate hemisphere of your brain in the serving sequence. That's when you change from an asymmetrical "half-brain" state, to a symmetrical "whole-brain" state. A state of equivalence between the real and the imaginary; balance between the past and the future. There's only one thing. It's a little strange at first — like serving in a daydream. But once you start using your whole brain to solve the problem of Positive Contact, you start "seeing" the solution. It's right in front of your eyes. All you have to do is look for it.

Index